COMMUNITY IN THE LORD

D0555856

COMMUNITY
IN THE LORD

PAUL HINNEBUSCH, O.P.

AVE MARIA PRESS
Notre Dame, Indiana 46556

Acknowledgments:

New Covenant, for permission to reprint "Whose Life Have I Touched?" February, 1975

Spiritual Life, for permission to reprint "Receiving God's Touch" Summer, 1974

Library of Congress Catalog Card Number: 75-14741

International Standard Book Number: 0-87793-099-6 (paper)
0-87793-098-8 (cloth)

Printed in the United States of America

Contents

Introduction

I was created by God to be known and lovingly accepted in joy by all my fellowmen. For only when others find joy in me, loving and appreciating me, can I acquire the healthy self-esteem necessary for my full growth as a human person and son of God. Only in achieving this human and spiritual growth can I give full glory to God my Father by becoming what he meant me to be: son of God in the Spirit of the Son, at home with my Father in Jesus my brother.

If I am to grow as son of God in the Son, I need to experience that God my Father loves me and rejoices in me. For I was made precisely for that purpose: to be known and appreciated by God, acknowledged by him as his son, filled by him with his love, penetrated through and through by the experience of this love poured out into my heart in the gift of his own Holy Spirit (Rm 5:5). My spiritual growth is my response to God's love and acceptance. It is my joyous response to the joy which God has in loving me as his son.

But God's joy in me, his loving acceptance and appreciation of me, is manifest to me in the love and joy and appreciation shown to me by my fellowmen who are filled with God's own Spirit of love. Only in community in the Lord Jesus can I fully respond to God my Father, only in the community of God's children can I be fully son of God. Only in a community of families and friends who are filled with the Holy Spirit can a Christian grow surely, swiftly and healthily in the life in the Spirit.

A main theme of this book, therefore, is response to God in Christian community.

To live in Christian community is to be *at home* with God our Father, and with his Son, Jesus, and with all our brothers and sisters in the Son; for Christian community is the family of God's children.

Home is where I am fully known and loved and received just as I am. It is where I am free to be completely myself without putting on acts to win approval. It is where I am appreciated and accepted with joy, and am encouraged by this appreciation to grow into my true self.

My whole destiny is to be fully at home with God. "In my Father's house there are many dwelling places" (Jn 14:20). In this imagery, Jesus is really telling us that God himself is our home. We are home at last when, in the Son, we are taken fully into "the Father's bosom" (Jn 1:18), the Father's inner life where the Son dwells. "Father, I will that where I am, they also may be" (Jn 17:24).

The three divine Persons are ever "at home" with one another in the life of the Holy Trinity, dwelling in each other in mutual love and knowledge and loving appreciation. To be at home in God is to be taken into this loving communion and joy which is the very life of the Holy Trinity.

In what follows, therefore, we shall show first what it means to be at home in Christian family life. Then, by analogy, we shall show what it means to be at home in Christian community, for community in the Lord is God's own family where we are all at home with one another.

Indeed, Christian community is but the extension and fullness of Christian family life.

We shall show also how loving response to those with whom we are at home is truly response to the Lord himself. For God's joy in loving us, and his loving acceptance of us, is revealed and given to us in the joyous love and appreciation shown to us by our fellowmen.

We shall show also what it means to be at home with God in prayer. This will be as much a book on prayer as on family and community. Only in the community of God's children, we said, can we be fully sons of God, at home with our Father. But to be fully son of God is to be in direct personal communion with the Father. We shall speak both of this direct personal communion with God and of the community setting for this communion. Community in the Lord is impossible without incessant prayer, for such community is the life together of God's children, who live ever in communion with their Father and with one another.

Both prayer and community are response to baptismal grace. In Baptism we are born anew as sons and daughters of God. Prayer is the recognition and acceptance of God our Father, in Christ his Son. Community is the recognition and acceptance of our brothers and sisters in the Lord, in consequence of our acceptance of God our Father. All this is the work of the Holy Spirit in us.

Not an Impossible Dream

Though we illustrate many points in this book by referring to what is happening in charismatic covenant communities, we are not implying that everyone should join such a community. There are many other forms of authentic Christian community. Therefore we have tried to limit ourselves to considering elements which we think are integral to every Christian community.

The book came into being chiefly as the fruit of my

reflection upon what I observed and experienced in the charismatic Community of God's Delight in Dallas, Texas. There is nothing in the book which does not reflect what is happening in that community. That is why we know that the book is not describing an impossible dream.

Perhaps those who have read my earlier books on religious community will say that this new book says little that I have not said before. That is partly true. But the fact that I was able to say the same things both before the beginning of the charismatic renewal and after my personal involvement in it verifies my contention that the charismatic renewal is in the mainstream of Christian spirituality as this has run through the centuries. The charismatic renewal is one of the many ways in which God's Holy Spirit is working today in bringing about the total restoration of God's people.

Any resemblance between this book and *Friendship in the Lord* is by no means coincidental.[1] The book is a sequel to that one, flowing from a new and deeper experience of the truths expressed in that, a deeper experience of at-homeness with friends in community, and of at-homeness with God in prayer, especially community prayer. If occasionally we take up again concepts from the earlier book, it is only to develop more fully the community aspects of the truths contained therein.

The opening section of the book, concerning fathers and sons, is not a digression from our theme of community. If to live in Christian community is to be fully "at home" with everyone in community, we must grasp what "home" is before we can understand community. And to know what home is, we must see the father's essential role in the home. Most of what we say about fathers, of course, applies to mothers as well.

---

1. Paul Hinnebusch, O.P., *Friendship in the Lord* (Notre Dame, Indiana 46556: Ave Maria Press), 1974.

Part 1

Community Is "Being at Home"

Chapter 1

The Listening Father

Son: Response to the Father

At a charismatic prayer meeting, a young mother told how she had learned a beautiful lesson about prayer while watching her husband bending over their tiny baby. The father was eager to hear the infant say "Daddy!" He kept bending over the cradle, repeating to the child, "Say 'Daddy,'" trying to call forth his son's cry of recognition and acceptance of him. The child was responding with his eyes and smile, but at best all he could say was something which the father thought was "Da!" The father was delighted with this much, and each day when he came home from work he would go to the cradle to try again.

Observing all this, the mother received a new insight into the words of St. Paul, "When we cry 'Abba, Father!' it is the Spirit himself bearing witness with our spirit that we are sons of God" (Rm 8:16). The heavenly Father is ever bending over us, calling forth our response to him in prayer, inspiring us by his Holy Spirit whom he has given into our hearts (Rm 5:5). Our prayer is still like the babbling of an infant. "Abba, Abba" seems to be all we can say. But the Father is pleased with this, and continues to invite us, gradually leading us to deeper recognition and acceptance of him as our loving Father.

A father is not fully father until he joyously acknowledges his son as his own, and lovingly accepts him into his care. A son is not fully son till he responds fully to his father, recognizing and acknowledging him as father. *Response is of the essence of sonship.* The father-son relationship is perfected only in the son's personal response to the father's loving acceptance of him. Fatherhood and sonship are thus a mutual personal relationship, completed only in mutual recognition and loving communion. So it is in our relationship with God. In its perfection, our Father-son relationship with him is a fullness of communion in love.

Speaking of our recognition and acceptance of God as our Father, St. Paul says, "The proof that you are sons is the fact that God has sent forth into our hearts the Spirit of his Son which cries out 'Abba, Father!' " (Gal 4:6). This cry of recognition is knowing God. "Now that you have come to know God, or rather to be known by him. . ." (Gal 4:9). In Paul's language, "to know" means more than intellectual knowledge. It is knowledge penetrated with love. It is acknowledgment, acceptance, appreciation.

But our acknowledgment of God is always a response to his acknowledgment of us: "Now that you have come to know God, or rather to be known by him." Only because we have been acknowledged as sons by God and have experienced his love for us poured out into our hearts in the gift of the Holy Spirit (Rm 5:5), have we come to know him, lovingly acknowledging him in the cry "Father" inspired by the Holy Spirit (Rm 8:15). In the very giving of the Spirit of adoption into my heart, God has lovingly known me as his son. My loving recognition of him as my father can only be in response to his love, in the power of his Spirit.

God's loving knowledge of me is given and manifested to me in Christ, his Son and Image. "As the Father knows me and I know the Father, so I know my own and my own know me" (Jn 10:14-15). "As the Father has loved me, so have I loved you. Abide in my love" (Jn 15:9). The Father knows and loves us in his beloved Son Jesus (Eph 1:5-6), and in this beloved Son we respond to the Father. We are sons in the Son. "No one comes to the Father but through me" (Jn 14:6).

"God destined us to be conformed to the image of his Son, that he might be the firstborn among many brothers" (Rm 8:29). Our growth in the image of the Son is a matter of ever-deepening recognition and response to the Father's love given to us in the Son. This love is poured out ever more fully into our hearts as the Lord Jesus takes ever fuller possession of us in his Holy Spirit of love. Christian prayer is simply coming to ever-fuller recognition and acceptance of what we are by reason of the baptismal grace in which we are born anew of water and the Spirit (Jn 5:5).

The Listening Father

When the woman at the prayer meeting told how her husband would bend over the cradle, trying to win his son's cry of recognition, she was speaking in the context of a larger message which God was giving through the various speakers at that meeting.

It was a glorious Sunday in May. The day had been brilliant with warm sunshine. The trees were clothed with fresh green leaves. Flowers were blooming everywhere. The mild and gentle air was sweet with a lovely fragrance. Therefore the first part of the prayer meeting was filled with praise and thanksgiving to God for all the wonders of his creation.

But, after a while, the Lord, pleased with his children,

responded to their praise of the wonders he accomplishes in nature, saying, "Yes, my children, I am beautiful in all this, but I am far more glorious in the wonderful things I am doing in you, my children. I find far more joy in you than in all the magnificent beauty of the whole created universe. For I delight in you just as I delight in Jesus, my beloved Son. You are my sons and daughters in him, and therefore in you I am well pleased."

It was then that the woman told how her husband would bend over the cradle, listening for their infant's cry.

A father is first of all a listener, listening for his child's cry of recognition. The heavenly Father, too, is ever bending his ear to us, listening for our cry to him in prayer. A child is also a listener, but only in response to parents who have first listened to him.

We often admit jokingly, but very truthfully, that the baby in the family is the real boss of the home. He is forever crying out for attention, and everyone listens to him. Everyone *obeys* his cries and responds to his needs.

This should be true, however, not only during the child's infancy, but throughout all his years of growth. There is a profound sense in which his father and mother should continue to obey the child until he has grown to full maturity.

The word "obey" means "to turn the ear toward," to listen attentively. Only a father who lovingly listens to his son can rightfully expect his son in turn to listen to him. A son fails to obey his father because the father has failed to listen to the son.

A good father is ever a good listener, ever lovingly attentive to his child. He listens not only for his son's first efforts to speak, hoping that the first word will be "Daddy!" He listens throughout the years to hear all his son's needs. He listens to the child's every effort to express himself in action as well as in word. He listens attentively to what his child is saying in his whole being and in all that he does.

In his whole person and in all his actions and words, the child is expressing his need for growth. He is expressing his powers and his potentialities which are crying out for fulfillment. The father listens to these needs, he detects these potentialities. And he obeys, he responds to what he has heard in the child. He gives what needs to be given to the child, and he lovingly calls forth from him, by word and encouragement, what can grow only from within. By his words of direction which he expects his son to obey, he calls forth the child's self-expression, he invites the development of his powers to speak, to walk, to do things, to make things, to think, to read, to write.

A father can lovingly call forth what is in the child only if he is lovingly attentive to the child to discern what is in him. He can rightfully expect obedience from his child only when whatever he asks the child to do corresponds to what is already groping for growth in the child. Thus, a father is not one who imposes his own arbitrary will upon his son, demanding obedience. He is one who first listens to his son's true needs, and then lovingly invites him, directs him, encourages him in accordance with these needs.

What the child is saying in his words and actions, and what the father listens to, is the child's true self, the self God meant him to be, the self which is the development and fulfillment of what God has planted in him. The father discerns what is of God in his son from what is from the evil in him, and encourages what is from God and disciplines what is of evil.

He learns what the child should be, not by studying himself, but by listening to all that is in the child. For though in one sense the son is the father's image, he is never an exact reproduction of his father. The child also has a mother, and he has a soul and spirit directly created by God and not of the parents' flesh and blood. Thus, though he is somewhat in his parents' image, at the same time he is a distinctive person in his own right, and not a replica stamped out forcibly like coins stamped out by a machine.

Therefore in giving directions to the child and requiring obedience of him, the father does not impose himself upon the child, nor does he impose upon him any preconceived notions of what this child should be. He forms his idea of what the child should be by obeying what he finds in the child, namely, all the wonderful potentialities that God has placed there. He rejoices in the treasures he finds in the child, because God has put them there to be lovingly nurtured and invited forth to full development.

A listening father, then, is one who appreciates his son. To appreciate someone is to recognize his value and rejoice in it with love. To appreciate a child means to reverence the child, for the value we recognize in him as a person is so sublime that it deserves nothing less than profound love and reverence.

All that we say about listening fathers is true, of course, about listening mothers and listening teachers. In the present book we speak more about listening fathers, because we fear that they are rarer than listening mothers, even though they are just as essential.

How I Became a Writer

As an author, I am often asked how I got my start in writing. In answer, I tell about an incident in my early childhood. I remember it vividly, because on that occasion my father responded to me with loving appreciation of my first poetic expression.

It was during my preschool days, and I was at home with my mother. I was watching a lovely snowfall, and, with a child's profound sense of wonder, I was enraptured with the mystery and beauty of what I saw. I began to sing, composing my own song. I spontaneously expressed my wonderment in very simple words set to a simple tune: "Winter out, snowing out, snowing on the porch roof." The slowly falling notes of the dreamy melody matched the gentle fall of the snowflakes. I was in perfect tune and rhythm with God's beautiful world, and, no doubt, with God himself who was silently at work in my heart. Little children are naturally contemplative, and are easily led to prayer.

I repeated my little refrain again and again, for I had not yet developed the art of variation. When my father came home for lunch, he heard me singing and noticed my rapture over the snowfall. He expressed his appreciation of what he heard and saw in me by giving me a penny—a fortune for a five-year-old in 1922!

That was the first and most precious royalties payment I have ever received, and it was paid in full, all at once. The penny was but a token of my father's loving joy in me, and his reverence for what he saw budding in me. At the lunch table he asked me to sing my poem for the whole family.

Later, one of my brothers scoffed at my composition and denied that it was a poem. Though he shook my self-confidence momentarily, I trusted more in my father's judgment than in his, and I withstood the attack. Critics come early in an author's life! My work really was a poem, for it was the expression of wonderment at the mysteries of God's magnificent creation.

In listening to my poem, my father had listened to me. He heard something far deeper than my simple words. His loving attention and appreciation gave me a new sense of worth, and encouraged my mental and spiritual growth.

About six years later when I was 11, my father again gave a loving impetus to my literary efforts. It was a rainy day in June, and I whiled away the time after school composing a little newspaper. I recorded in headlines some unusual events which had taken place in the family that day. I drew a cartoon, and I filled in the rest of the pages with jokes. I didn't trouble to show my newspaper to anyone, because I had composed it merely for my own amusement. It got lost among some papers on our library table, and I forgot all about it.

About a week later my father came across it, and read it with deep appreciation. He came to me, and encouraged me to continue the newspaper. At once I began the second edition, and for more than two years brought out an issue every week. I called it *The Harem Scarem Weekly*. Before long, every member of our large family was reading the paper avidly, and contributing news items, comic strips, and other features. The little project did much to improve our home and deepen our family life.

And all because my father had lovingly listened to what he heard growing in me, and, by the sun of his appreciation, helped it to blossom and bear fruit.

A few years before this, in my second year in school, one day my teacher pointed to a picture on the wall, and asked the class to write a story about it. She was so pleased with my composition that she called my mother, and told her to encourage me to continue writing. My mother lovingly relayed this message to me, and from then on I always took delight in writing the compositions assigned by my teachers, even when the theme was the perennial one for the first day of each school year, "How I Spent My Vacation."

Every true father, or mother, or teacher, is an obedient listener, bending his ear toward the needs and powers crying out in the child's whole being. A child too is a listener, responding to his parents who have first listened to him. My father never had any problems of disobedience and rebellion with me, because he always listened to me. I loved to work side by side with him in our garden and in various projects we undertook together for the upkeep of our house and home. I was at home with him, because he knew how to listen to me, and how to let me experience the joy of using the powers and talents God had given me.

A father is one who takes away fear. When a child is learning to walk, for example, his fear of falling disappears because his father is lovingly near and watching, inviting a courageous stepping forth, and ready to catch him if he falls. So too a father who lovingly takes time to encourage his child to make and do things takes fear from the child's heart, and instills in him the courage and self-confidence that comes from experiencing his ability to do things.

Too many parents do too many things for their children, and so the children do not grow up to be capable and self-confident persons. There was one thing my mother did for me a little longer than was necessary. When I was a tot, she dressed me every morning. But one morning she was not there, and my grandfather was my baby-sitter. And he really did sit, ignoring me as he read the morning paper. I looked at him with my clothes in my hands, expecting him to dress me. No response. So I set about dressing myself. To my pleasant surprise and joy I found I was able to do it. Thus I experienced a new sense of mastery over my little world! I came to know myself in a new way as a distinctive individual, a unique person in my own right, no longer totally dependent upon others.

It is important that parents let their children do things on their own, and not baby them too long. A child experiences his power to do things because his parents have lovingly let him do things, and have shown their loving appreciation of whatever he did. It is of the nature of true fatherhood and motherhood to take away fear and inspire love and confidence in their children.

Because my own father's love and reverence for me called forth the best that was in me, I loved him, and he never had to force his will upon me. Therefore I had no fear of his authority, though his authority was always lovingly evident. I always held him in deep reverence, but there was no fear in this relationship.

That is how it is with God our Father. Just as my earthly father took away all fear from my heart, so from God in heaven "we did not receive a spirit of slavery leading us back into fear, but a spirit of adoption through which we cry out, 'Abba!' (that is, 'Father!')" (Rm 8:15). I have never had any difficulty identifying with these words of St. Paul, because I had an earthly father who was a true image of God: a presence and manifestation of the Father in heaven.

Chapter 2

Home Is Where Everyone Listens

Home is where I am appreciated as the true self I am, the person God meant me to be. It is where I am held precious as a magnificent work of God's love. It is where I am reverenced as a person made in God's own image and likeness, a person existing in my own right. I am not to be molded according to mere whims and fancies of my parents, but am to be allowed to grow in the way God meant me to be.

For as a child I am not the property of my parents, I am not to be used by them as they will. They have no authority arbitrarily to impose their own will upon me. They must search out God's will for me. They must listen to my whole being, they must search my heart to see what God has put there, and what God is doing there. They have authority only to invite forth lovingly from me the potentialities which God has placed in me. Their authority is exercised properly only when it is love's invitation and love's guidance to become what I ought to be in God's plan. When necessary, of course, authority is also love's correction, and even love's coercion.

I can grow properly only when I am lovingly listened to and appreciated, and encouraged to express what is best in me. To listen to me is to be attentive to my whole being, and to receive lovingly all that I am communicating in everything that I am, and do, and say. The listener, however, must be able to distinguish the cry of my true self from the cry of my false self. He must discern what stems from sin in me, and what stems from God's Spirit.

He who does not listen to me is saying that I am not worth listening to, and therefore he is telling me that I am not lovable or worthy of esteem. If I am not lovingly listened to, I cannot have a healthy self-esteem. If I lack self-esteem, I am paralyzed with fears, I am afraid to do anything, and therefore I cannot grow.

Only Love Can Listen

Listening, however, is the attitude not only of parents toward their children. Home is where everyone is a listener, and everyone is listened to. Husband and wife listen to each other with loving and perceptive hearts. On an adult level, they understand each other's needs, and appreciate each other's gifts and potentialities. By this mutual esteem and appreciation, they invite continuing growth from each other.

Only if I love can I listen. For only if I love am I interested and concerned enough to listen attentively. If I do not listen, I do not really love. Only if I am lovingly interested in the other and concerned about him and attentive to him can I really hear and understand. Thus only love is capable of listening and understanding.

To love is to go out of myself as the center of interest, and to make the loved one the focus of attention. Only if he is the center of interest and attention can I fully listen to him undistracted by self-interest, and hear what he is really saying. Love listens and understands, and through listening and understanding, loves the more.

Listening is but the action of my cherishing love, love which grows in esteem and reverence for the one I love the more I listen to him. For if I listen and watch lovingly, I discover ever-new beauty in the loved one, and because I appreciate and cherish it, this beauty grows, invited to full bloom by the warm sun of my loving appreciation.

Loving listening is essential in all human relationships: in the family, in the community, in society at large. To love and to listen I must die to my sinful self-centeredness. I must learn to forget self in my loving concern for the other. I must learn to be fully present to others through my love and concern.

Obeying One Another

It is not enough for me to listen to others and hear what they are saying. I must also *obey* them. That is, I must *respond* to what I hear, and let it influence my ways of acting. Only if I act upon what I hear can I succeed in establishing loving relationships with those whom I listen to and hear.

On this point, modern homes and communities could learn much from the ancient Christian monks. The monks obeyed not only the ruling authorities in their communities. They obeyed one another. In the Rule of St. Benedict, for example, we read, "The precious gift of obedience should be rendered by all not only to the father abbot, but the brothers should also obey each other, knowing that this path of obedience shall lead them to God" (Chapter 71).

The word "obey," we said, derives from words meaning "to turn the ear toward, to listen." To obey one another means to listen always to one another, to be ever attentive to the needs and just wishes of others, and to respond to these needs and wishes in preference to one's own desires

and plans. "Let each of you look not only to his own interests, but also to the interests of others" (Phil 2:4).

There is a twofold reason for this. First, the monks
knew that the very nature of Christ's love in us takes us out
of self to live for others. Christian life is community, not
individualism. Community is possible only when we hear
and obey the needs and joys of one another. "Rejoice
with those who rejoice, weep with those who weep" (Rm
12:15).

Secondly, the monks were deeply aware that, in contra-
diction to Christ's love, all of us tend to be very self-
centered and concerned primarily with our own interests.
Therefore, we must make a deliberate effort to go out of
ourselves to make others the focus of our love and concern.
A very effective way of doing this, the monks found, was
always to obey others, no matter who they were, whether
the abbot or the very least of the brothers. They cultivated
the custom of refusing to listen to their own self-centeredness, responding instead to every call that came to them in
the needs and requests of others. They were very conscious
of the Lord's words, "As you did it to one of the least of
these my brothers, you did it to me" (Mt 25:40).

Thus they became ever more delicately sensitive to one
another, and less and less wrapped up in self. Only thus
could they live in true Christian community. Listening and
responding is of the essence of community in the Lord.

This mutual obedience is not simply a monastic custom.
It is of the very nature of Christ's life and love in us. It
should be a basic principle in every Christian home and in
every Christian community. "Let each of us please his
neighbor for his good, to build him up; for Christ did not
please himself" (Rm 15:2). Every Christian is essentially
a listener to others, and quick to respond to them lovingly.
A listening and responsive heart is indispensable for true
community.

Only where we live in mutual obedience can we be truly at home with one another. For I am at home only where listening hearts accept me lovingly, appreciate me fully, reverence me deeply, and thus call forth from me in turn a love which takes me out of my self-centeredness and self-pity, a love in which I am sensitive to the needs of others, and turned toward them in loving concern.

Listening Hearts

In a special way, of course, parents of families, leaders of communities, and rulers of peoples need listening hearts. When Solomon became king of God's people, he prayed for a listening heart:

> Now, O Lord my God, you have made your servant king in place of my father David, though I am a mere child, unskilled in leadership. And I am here in the midst of your people, the people of your choice, too many to be numbered or counted. Give therefore your servant *a heart with skill to listen,* so that he may govern your people justly and distinguish good from evil. For who is equal to the task of governing this great people of yours?
>
> The Lord was well pleased that Solomon had asked for this, and he said to him, "Because you have asked for this, and not for long life for yourself, or for wealth, or for the lives of your enemies, but have asked for discernment to understand what is right, I grant your request. I give you a heart so wise and so understanding that there has been none like you before your time, nor will be after you" (1 Kgs 3:7-12).

Solomon asked for a listening heart. To whom did he want to listen? To God, and to his people. He wanted to listen to God, because he wanted to discern God's will for his people, distinguishing right from wrong, good from evil. He wanted to listen to his people, because he wanted to distinguish right for them and in them: in their daily lives, in settling their disputes, in establishing God's justice among them.

He wanted to be able to discern which of their desires sprang from the evil in them, and which sprang from the good which God was working in them. Thus, in the story immediately following his prayer for a listening heart, Solomon discerns the evil in the heart of the woman who tries to steal the other woman's child, and the good in the heart of the true mother of the child (1 Kgs 3:16-28). And he makes a firm decision accordingly.

A person in authority, a head of a family or a community, is one who must discern and decide. He must make decisions, right decisions. He can do this only if he has a listening heart, a heart which listens to God and to the hearts of his people. He listens to God in prayer and he listens to God working in the lives of his people. He discerns in them what is from God, distinguishing it from what is from sin and selfishness. He makes firm decisions accordingly and implements them. A peaceful and orderly family or community is not possible where the head of the group has no listening heart, or abdicates his responsibility for making and carrying out right decisions.

Loving listening is essential in all human relationships. Love listens and understands, and through listening and understanding, loves the more. O Lord, in all our relationships give us hearts with skill to listen. Give us loving hearts, responsive hearts!

Chapter 3

Community Is "Being at Home"

Community is simply the fullness of home. Home, we said, is where I am known and loved, listened to and appreciated. Therefore it is where I am free to be my true self. Community, as the fullness of home, is where I am listened to and accepted, appreciated and loved, not just by my immediate family, but by all the fellowmen with whom I share my life. It is where I live not simply in my family's love, but in everyone's love. It is where I am at home in everyone's love and acceptance.

Home and community begin with two. Jesus describes Christian community as being together in his name. "Where two or three are gathered together in my name, there am I in the midst" (Mt 18:20). "Two in my name" is already community in Christ.

Two in the Lord—husband and wife—is the basic Christian community. These two, however, are completed only in a family of children who are lovingly accepted. Then it is really home. Home is where God's children are lovingly accepted into the world.

But home, in the sense of one couple and their children, is not enough. Home in this sense is incomplete because each family is completed only through its acceptance and integration into the larger human community. The family is not sufficient unto itself. My fullest growth can be achieved only in relationships which extend beyond the home and reach out into the whole community of mankind.

For no one person can call forth from me all the multiple riches which God has put into my being like a seed to be developed. Nor am I of myself rich enough in gifts and personality to call forth the development of all the gifts of the persons I love. These persons need relationships with others besides me. To reach our fullest growth as persons we need a whole complex of relationships with persons other than those in our family; we need community.

Different persons call forth different facets of my being. Whether I am daughter or son, sister or brother, wife or husband, I need further relationships which extend outside my home. Not only I as an individual, but my home and family as a small community must be fully integrated into the larger human community.

The mother of a family, for example, when she was still a child responded first to her parents, and then to her brothers and sisters; then to her playmates and teachers and schoolmates; and then to many other persons, before she met her husband and responded to him and he to her. Before she could have a healthy and full relationship with her fiance and then to him as husband, she had to be able to relate to adult persons of both sexes in a variety of ways. But all of this was possible only in a healthy community.

As mother of her family she now responds to her children, and thus she continues to grow as a person. The human heart, however, is too great to be focused only on these few. Therefore, especially as her children grow up and no longer require the fullness of her attention, her heart reaches out more and more to others in the community, responding to the needs of the poor, the sick, the helpless, the sinful, the addicted. In all these relationships she continues to grow (cf. Prv 31).

Only in and with the help of the larger community can she and her husband provide all that their children need. Only in the midst of a multitude of human relationships in a strong community life can their adolescent children learn to relate to many people of both sexes in all the facets of life. Such a variety of relationships is a necessary preparation for marriage.

Without many such relationships, preparation for marriage would be only the narrow and inadequate "one to one" relationship between one boy and one girl "going steady." Because these two have limited their relationships too much to each other, they have not learned the multitude of human relationships necessary for a full life, and only too often have learned to relate to each other only on the biological-sexual level. They have been too much alone with each other, and so their human growth has been hindered.

These are only a few of the reasons why all of us need to be at home not only in a family, but also in a larger community. To be in community is to be at home in a network of loving human relationships.

Since a home, a family, is a loving relationship in which everyone listens to and responds to and receives and appreciates everyone else, a home or family is integrated into the larger human family or community only when these loving relationships of listening and appreciating are opened to all others within our ordinary sphere of life. Community is simply the extension to others of these family relationships of listening and appreciating. Community is being at home in the loving appreciation of everyone.

The gospel presents some more profound and more

sublime reasons why the family is completed only through its complete integration into a larger fraternal community, and why, in a very true sense, Christian community is the extension and fullness of Christian family life.

In Baptism we are all reborn of water and the Holy Spirit as sons of God. Therefore the baptismal community, community in the Lord, is God's own family, where everyone is at home with everyone else as true brothers and sisters. Christian community is essentially fraternal, in the fullest meaning of that word. Being "at home" with our fellowmen as brothers and sisters in the Lord is of the very nature of the Christian life.

This is salvation. Salvation is community, for salvation is the health and wholeness of man. Man is person, and to be fully person is to live in fraternal relationship with others in awareness and love. Man is truly man only when he lives in loving relationships with God and his fellowmen. Thus man is essentially family and community, and salvation is the healing and perfecting of the relationships which knit together the community of mankind. Salvation is man's loving communion in the Lord with God his Father, in loving communion with all his brothers and sisters in the Lord.

Home, then, is incomplete until it is integrated into a larger community which is itself a fullness of all the truly fraternal elements of home life.

Part 2

Baptismal Responsibility for Community

Chapter 4

Baptism: Commitment to Community

In Baptism, we enter into the new and eternal covenant in the blood of Jesus. Commitment to Jesus in this covenant is necessarily commitment to community. Therefore Baptism brings the responsibility of building Christian community.

For our baptismal covenant with Christ is a commitment not only to God, but to all his people. It is the filial response, in Jesus, to the love which the Father pours out into our hearts, when he adopts us as his sons and daughters in the Holy Spirit. It is loving surrender to our Father's will to save us as a community of brothers and sisters in Christ Jesus his Son.

Thus, Baptism is a commitment not only to the Lord Jesus but to all our brothers and sisters in the Lord. Our relationship with Jesus is truly a family covenant. When the Lord said, on the day of his resurrection, "I am ascending to my Father and your Father, to my God and your God" (Jn 20:17), he was reexpressing the traditional covenant formula of the Old Testament, "I will be their God, and they shall be my people" (Jer 31:33). Jesus thus tells us that this God, his Father, is now our Father too, and therefore the new covenant people is God's own family, bound together in covenant love.

Because we are God's own family, sons and daughters of God, brothers and sisters in the Lord, Christian community is characterized by truly fraternal relationships and family virtues. It is truly the family of God's children in which everyone is at home in everyone's love.

Christian Covenant Love

Already in the Old Covenant, the qualities of the covenant love binding God and his people together were essentially family qualities. The steadfast love and faithfulness, so characteristic of God in his covenant relationship with his people, were the traditional Hebrew family virtues. These same virtues were expected of all God's people in all their relationships with one another in the community of Israel.

The family virtues were summed up in two words, *hesed we emet*. These Hebrew words are so rich in meaning that no two words in any other language can adequately translate them. They have been variously translated as "steadfast love and faithfulness," "loving-kindness and fidelity," "love and loyalty." They express the sum total of all the qualities of the ideal family relationship, and mean such things as an undying love, loving-kindness, family loyalty, faithfulness, truth, trust, confidence in one another, loyal love, compassionate love, loving mercy, forgiveness.

These family qualities had to be shown in all relationships with everyone in the Israelite covenant community, for the community was God's own family. "Steadfast love and faithfulness" are practically a description of the covenant obligation. They are true above all of God in his covenant relationship with his people. They are to be imitated by his people in their relationships with him and with one another.

The Book of Ruth is built up entirely around this theme of steadfast love and family loyalty. By her marriage, Ruth had become a member of Naomi's family, and nothing could persuade her to abandon her bereaved mother-in-law. The calm and profound attachment of Ruth's loyal heart is the human perfection of covenant love. Her loyalty to her deceased husband's family leads Ruth to seek out Boaz, so that he in turn, as nearest of kin, might express the same family loyalty by marrying the widowed Ruth, and thus continue the family.

Loyal family love has all the qualities of God's own steadfast love in keeping his covenant with Abraham. This is clear in the story of Abraham's servant sent to seek a bride for Abraham's son, Isaac (Gn 24). The sign that Rebekah is the perfect bride to continue Abraham's family is the loving-kindness she exercises toward the servant in giving him a drink, watering his camels, and offering him hospitality with her family (Gn 24:17-27).

Because Abraham's family is God's own covenant family, the qualities God expects within the family of Abraham's descendants are the very same covenant qualities which God himself expresses toward this people. Thus, Abraham's servant sees Rebekah's loving-kindness toward himself as a sign that God is showing steadfast love to Abraham, by providing for Isaac a wife endowed with these basic family and covenant virtues (Gn 24:12-14).

Thus, the Hebrew family virtues have a divine quality about them. They are patterned upon and they express God's own family relationship with his chosen people. In exercising covenant love, God's people live in his own image and likeness.

Because loving-kindness and steadfast loyalty were the primary obligation assumed in making the covenant with

God, the words "covenant" and "steadfast love" became practically synonyms. In biblical speech the two words were often yoked together as two ways of saying the same thing: "the faithful God who *keeps covenant and steadfast love* with those who love him and keep his commandments" (Dt 7:9).

Concrete Expression of the Covenant

That this covenant love reaches out beyond the immediate blood relationship, and embraces even rivals and enemies, is manifest in the friendship of David and Jonathan. These two were from rival families, for Saul, Jonathan's father, was bent upon destroying David, because David seemed destined to take the throne away from Saul and his family.

David and Jonathan make a covenant of friendship, and agree to express God's own covenant qualities in this friendship. David says to Jonathan, "Deal with me, your servant, in loving-kindness, for you have brought your servant into *a covenant of the Lord*" (1 Sm 20:8). The covenant is inspired by the Lord himself! Jonathan, fore-seeing how David will one day have the throne which Jonathan himself should have inherited, says to David, "If I am still alive, show me *the Lord's loyal love,* that I may not die; and do not cut off your loyalty from my house forever" (1 Sm 20:14). After Jonathan's death, David, faithful to his covenant of friendship in the Lord, seeks out Jonathan's heir, "that I may show *God's kindness* to him" (2 Sm 9:3).

The covenant of love made by David and Jonathan thus had all the qualities of God's own covenant with his people, Israel. The brotherly love of these two, who might otherwise have been bitter rivals, foreshadowed the total reconciliation of all mankind as brothers in the new covenant in Christ's blood.

Because it expressed all the qualities of God's covenant with his people, Israel, the covenant of friendship between these two men was their way of living together, their sharing in Israel's covenant with God himself. It was a concrete way of expressing in their personal lives their people's covenant with the Lord. Man's covenant with God can be lived only in everyday loving human relationships with one's fellowmen.

So, too, Christian Baptism, in which we enter into the new and eternal covenant with God in the blood of Jesus, brings to each of us the impelling responsibility to develop concrete, down-to-earth ways of expressing this covenant in our everyday human relationships with one another. We must build a covenant community in which we express our covenant love.

Covenant love is love of God and love of neighbor, and love can be lived only in the concrete. If I say I love everyone, and do nothing about it, then in reality I love no one. I must respond in a practical way to those whom I love. The Old Testament always spoke of "doing" covenant love. Love goes into action. Love is doing something for the loved ones. It is responding to their neediness and emptiness, or it is rejoicing in their fullness and happiness. When this loving response is mutual, the result is communion in covenant love.

Our baptismal covenant with Christ is unfulfilled if our covenant love is not embodied in a lasting way of life, involving concrete deeds of love for one another.

We, therefore, have the responsibility to build a community which will be the concrete workable embodiment in daily life of the eternal covenant we have made with God in Baptism. By embodying our covenant love in a concrete way of life we build up the body of Christ. Like a human body, Christ's body, the Christian community, is an organic organization of Christian life in which each member fulfills his proper function for the good of the whole. Therefore, throughout the rest of this book we shall frequently refer to Christian community as the body of Christ, or simply the body.

Building such a community is our baptismal responsibility. Since every grace and gift of God entails a responsibility, the supreme responsibility comes with the supreme Gift, the Holy Spirit, the Spirit of adoption as sons given to us in Baptism. In this Gift, God's own love is poured out into our hearts, God's own life is given to us. God's love given to us calls for our wholehearted love in response, response to God our Father, and response to all our brothers and sisters in God's life.

Thus, the supreme responsibility, coming with the supreme Gift given in Baptism, is the responsibility to live together in loving communion with God our Father, and to build fraternal community in love.

In the responsibility to build Christian community, all our other human responsibilities are summed up and contained, for the responsibility to live in communion with God can be fulfilled only by living in community with our brothers and sisters in the Lord; and community is possible only where every human responsibility of love and justice and cooperation is fulfilled. Only in community can these responsibilities be fulfilled, for they are only so many aspects of covenant love. Our baptismal covenant with Jesus, then, brings the responsibility to build community in the Lord.

Chapter 5

Family, Community, and World Salvation

In building community by the power of Christ, we bring about the salvation of mankind in universal brotherhood.

Each one of us, by reason of Baptism, is a missionary, with the responsibility of continuing Christ's own mission of salvation. This is a mission to build community, and can be carried out only in community cooperation. The goal of the mission is the fullness of community in the Lord.

For salvation consists in universal brotherhood. Salvation is the reconciliation and unity of mankind as sons of God (Col 1:13-22). These sons live in the presence of God their Father (Eph 1:4). They are united under the headship of Jesus Christ, the Beloved Son (Eph 1:9). He is the firstborn of many brothers (Rm 8:29). Therefore, salvation is the community of all of God's children, united as brothers and sisters in the Lord, in communion with God their Father.

The whole world can and must be changed from a world organized in sin and selfishness, its peoples closed to God and alienated from one another. It must be transformed into God's world of love and universal brotherhood, "knit together in love" (Col 2:2).

But all this can be achieved only as a community of communities. The work of salvation is a work of building community in the Lord, and Baptism gives each Christian the responsibility to join in this work. The fullness of salvation is the fullness of community in Jesus. Salvation is already at work among us and is being achieved to the extent that fraternal unity in Christ exists in authentic Christian communities.

These communities manifest the power of salvation, the power of Christ's Holy Spirit of love, and draw others to enter into salvation by entering into community with the Lord. Such communities are actually bringing about salvation by building themselves up in covenant love as the body of Christ, by the power of the Holy Spirit.

Obviously, the salvation of the world is a cooperative work, and can be achieved only by Christian communities. Such communities can be built only by groups cooperating with other groups, and by the cooperation of individuals within each of these groups, so that the whole community is a living body, the Lord's body.[1]

The Role of Families in Salvation

Since the basic unit of human and Christian community is the family, families have a fundamental and exceedingly important role to play in the salvation of the world. Mankind cannot be saved in universal brotherhood except as a family of families of God's children. The universal brotherhood of mankind is possible only if everywhere in the world there is local brotherhood, uniting families and other in-

---

1. In the charismatic Community of God's Delight there is a variety of groups, each engaged in a specific ministry within the community; e.g., the youth ministry, the children's ministry, the music ministry, the ministry of leadership exercised by the elders, etc.

dividuals in local communities, with each of these local brotherhoods fully integrated with other brotherhoods into the universal brotherhood of mankind. There will be universal brotherhood only when there is authentic brotherhood in each individual home, and each home is fully integrated into true community.

If the very foundation of the world's salvation is Christian families united into Christian communities in covenant love, the world cannot be saved unless families fulfill their baptismal responsibility to cooperate fully in building Christian communities.

No family can fashion integral Christians by its own resources alone. An integral Christian is one who is fully integrated into the whole Christian community, and into all mankind, and at every stage of his development from infancy onward this process of integration must be under way. Hence the family in which he grows must be integrated fully into the larger community.

Each family fulfills its part in Christ's mission to build community, and thus save the world, by doing two things. First, it must bring about order and unity within itself. Secondly, it must work for its own total integration into the order of the whole community. These two must go on simultaneously, mutually influencing each other.

The starting point for setting our personal lives and our families in order is recognition and acceptance of the Lord's personal headship over our persons, our families, our communities. Therefore, in preparing for charismatic covenant communities, the first thing the Holy Spirit does is form prayer communities. The fundamental prayer of these communities is praise and adoration of Jesus as Lord. Once Jesus is firmly accepted as Lord in these people's lives, he quickly establishes them in ever-deepening community with one another.

When the father, head of a family, is in right order with

God through his obedience to Jesus as Lord and head, his family in turn is quickly set in order under the father's headship, and the healing of family relationships is brought about. But families are able to fulfill their mission in the greater community of mankind only by integrating into communities of covenant love with other families and other persons whose lives they touch each day. Thus the healing of human relationships begins to spread far and wide. From these communities, peace flows out like a river over the whole earth. Eventually the whole world will be and must be changed from a world organized in selfishness and sin into a new creation, God's world of covenant love and universal brotherhood.

Just as the family is the basic unit in the community of mankind, so the father is the firm foundation of family. If the father is not what he should be, the family cannot be right, and all human community is weakened.

Fulfilling Responsibility for Community

To fulfill the baptismal responsibility for building community, each one in the new covenant with Christ embodies covenant love in all his relationships with others. Each person does this in keeping with his own specific vocation, his own life-situation and circumstances. He loves in a concrete practical way those whom God has given him to love. This love consists largely in doing the loving services he renders to others in the community.

A child lives the spiritual covenant by responding to those who love him, returning their love in daily life situations, loving his parents, his brothers and sisters, his teachers and classmates, his friends and neighbors. He expresses this love through service within the home, the school, the community, in obedience to his parents and teachers.

When he comes to adulthood, he seeks and finds his adult way of living the covenant with Christ, loving those whom God has given him to love and serve. His concrete way of embodying his covenant with God in loving and practical human relationships will be determined by his particular vocation in life; for each one's way of participating in the covenant is always a response to a special personal call from God. Each has his unique vocation within the great call to the covenant in Christ's blood.

If a person is called to Christian marriage, then his marriage is his basic way of embodying his covenant with Christ in a practical way of life. In his married life, he embodies and expresses Christ's own love for the Church, for Christ has poured his own love into the man's heart, so that he can love his wife and family with the Lord's own love; just as David and Jonathan were loyal to each other with the Lord's own loyalty. Just as a husband's love for his wife is an embodiment of Christ's own love for her, so her love for her husband embodies Christ's love for him.

The commitment of husband and wife to each other in their marriage covenant is as serious and binding as is their baptismal commitment to God himself in the blood of Christ, for their marriage is their basic concrete way of living and expressing their covenant with the Lord in his body, the Church. It is their fundamental way of contributing to the building up of that body of Christ, the Christian community.

Priests and Religious as Builders of Community

The following paragraphs are meant for all readers of this book, not just for priests and religious.

Things similar to what we have just said about marriage are true of the priesthood and of the religious life.

The sacrament of Holy Orders, like that of Matrimony, is a continuation and completion of the sacrament of Baptism. By Baptism we are incorporated into Christ's body. All the other sacraments continue the building up of this body, the community. Thus, the sacraments of Matrimony and Orders empower Christians for specific functions in the Lord's body. Therefore, both matrimonial and priestly obligations are rooted in the universal baptismal responsibility to build community in the Lord. The specific workable way for a man in Holy Orders to live his baptismal covenant is by fulfilling the responsibilities he assumes in accepting the sacrament of Orders.

In an analogous way, the obligations of persons in religious communities are also rooted in Baptism. Profession of vows in a religious community is a commitment not only to Christ, but to all the members of the religious community and, indeed, to all the members of the Church. It is a commitment to a concrete specific way of living in community the baptismal covenant in the Lord's blood.

Religious profession is sanctioned and consecrated by the Church as a viable embodiment of the baptismal covenant, a permanent workable way of living in Christ's body and building it up in love. When the Church accepts an individual's religious profession, it confirms that individual's divine call to live his baptismal responsibilities in the specific way to which he has committed himself by religious profession. Since the Church ratifies each religious profession as a vocation in Christ's body, the covenant of religious profession derives its binding force from the baptismal covenant in which it is rooted, and which it expresses in a striking way.

By the very nature of the religious life, religious have always been community builders. Indeed "community" has been an integral element of the very definition of the religious life in church law. Today more than ever it is essential that religious communities be not closed in upon themselves, but fully integrated into the larger Christian community in openness and exchange.

Throughout the history of the Church, whenever religious communities were at their best and in their full fervor, they were open to the rest of God's people, with a vital influence flowing back and forth. Monasteries were centers of hospitality and of works of charity, of spirituality, and of Christian culture and civilization. Mendicant friars went out into the midst of the people in the cities and towns, preaching the gospel and witnessing to Christian living by their fraternal communities. Their very name "friars" meant "brothers." More modern religious communities have also been apostolic, rendering wonderful service to the whole people of God through their educational work and other charismatic graces of love and mercy.

There are two basic reasons for the failure of many religious communities in recent years to be as powerful as they should be in the work of building mankind into universal brotherhood in Christ.

First, in many communities there has been neglect of community prayer. Or even when the religious do pray together, their prayer has not had the full charismatic vitality which it usually had in the days of a religious community's first fervor.

Secondly, too many religious communities have failed to be fully open to the larger Christian community in the new ways required by the new needs of our times. They have been so narrowly concentrated in the old ways of doing things that they have been blind to the new needs of their fellowmen and new avenues of openness to them. A Christian community can never be completely closed in upon itself.

The needs of mankind today are the most fundamental needs of human life. Alienation, isolation, broken homes, broken relationships in all of human life have produced a lonely mankind. People need community, loving human relationships, respect for persons, respect for life itself. These are needs which can be met only by a full restoration of Christian family life in communities of families. Often enough religious communities have broken down because so many of the persons they have received into the community were incapable of living in community, because they had never found loving appreciation and mutual communion in the more basic community, the family and the local community. Greater care than ever therefore has to be taken to see to it that religious communities are true families of brothers and sisters in the Lord, with more attention to human love and warmth.

Religious communities in our times should be integrated into the total Christian community in such a way that they will not only contribute to the restoration of fully fraternal Christian life among their fellowmen but will themselves benefit from fraternal exchange with the rest of God's people. Perhaps the way that groups of consecrated celibates are springing up in the midst of charismatic communities as an integral part of these communities, in full vital exchange with them, contains a lesson for the older religious communities.

Chapter 6

Start With What You Are

Since salvation consists in communion with God in Christian community, only community can save the world, and community *will* save the world.

Such salvation looks completely impossible if we consider the seemingly endless misery and confusion in human life throughout the world today. The task of building a world according to God's will seems so absolutely hopeless that we are tempted to give up in discouragement and do nothing at all about it.

But the task is not at all impossible and is in no way hopeless, for the risen Lord is at work in the hearts of men by the power of his Holy Spirit. It is he who is raising up new communities everywhere. The Lord did not die in vain, and he is present in our midst completing his work of salvation. When we surrender to the Lord and his Spirit and let them form us into communities of love, we become ever more powerful in changing the whole world. With firm hope and complete conviction, Vatican II wrote:

The effort to establish universal brotherhood is not a hopeless one. For Jesus is Lord and head of all human life. He has entered the world's history as a perfect man, taking that history up into himself and bringing it under his headship. Appointed Lord by his Father at the resurrection and given all power in heaven and on earth, Christ is now at work in the hearts of men through the power of his Spirit. . . . Jesus has revealed to us that God is love, and that the new command of love is the basic law of human fulfillment, and therefore of the world's transformation *(Constitution of the Church in the Modern World,* 38).

"You Give Them Something to Eat"

That our task of renewing the world in love is not a hopeless one is asserted with striking beauty in the gospel story of the multiplication of the loaves. When great crowds had followed Jesus into a desert place and had been listening to him all day, the disciples urged Jesus to dismiss the crowds so that they could go into the villages to buy food (Mk 6:36).

But Jesus said, *you* feed them, "You give them something to eat" (6:37). The disciples responded: That's a hopeless task! "Are we to go and spend two hundred days' wages for bread to feed them?" (6:37).

Jesus replied: Start with what you have! "How many loaves have you?" (6:38). They looked and found five loaves and two fish. Jesus blessed these, broke them, and gave them back to the disciples to distribute (Lk 9:16). "And everyone ate till he had enough; and they gathered together twelve baskets of broken pieces that were left over" (Lk 9:17).

When the disciples obeyed Jesus' command to feed the multitude with what they had, Jesus blessed their efforts, and the whole crowd had enough to eat and much to spare.

If then we are tempted to shirk our responsibility for the overwhelming multitude of broken homes, of people alienated from one another in sin, of people poor and destitute and oppressed because of the greed of others, of people finding relief from their loneliness in drugs and drink and sex abuse—if we shirk our responsibility for all this as individuals and as community, and excuse ourselves saying, "The task is so hopeless that there is no use starting," Jesus witnesses against us in the living word of this gospel story, and says, "Start with what you have!"

St. John the Almsgiver, bishop of Alexandria in Egypt in the seventh century, well understood the meaning of the miracle of the five loaves. At the time of the Persian invasion of Western Asia, when Egypt was flooded with refugees from Palestine, the task of caring for all these hungry and homeless people seemed hopeless. But John said to the deacons whom he put in charge of the poor: "Even if all the beggars in the world came running to Alexandria for alms, they would not be able to exhaust the inexhaustible treasures of God, who has mercifully made me the unworthy dispenser of his goods."

Start With What You Have

The inexhaustible mercy of Christ has said to us: You yourselves take care of the sick, the poor, the distressed, the sinful. In reply to our protests of hopelessness in the face of the task his reply is: Start where you are, with what you have. Heal your daily human relationships in true community. I will bless your efforts until the whole world has had enough to eat, has been clothed and sheltered, has been healed of its sin and sickness, and has been "knit together in love" (Col 2:2) in universal brotherhood.

It is not enough to give what you have to relieve the

sufferings of others. Giving all that you have presupposes the gift of your very self. You must give all that you are.

Only in the gift of our whole persons to one another in brotherly community have we given enough. Only if our very selves are given in full fraternal love to our brothers and sisters in the Lord can there be authentic Christian community and universal brotherhood. Only in this way can we live our Baptism completely, and only thus can the world be saved. If Christian community has not yet changed the world, it is because too few of us have really been brother or sister to the brothers and sisters for whom Christ died (1 Cor 8:11).

The more completely I give myself, and am integrated into full Christian community with those whom God has given me to love in a special way, the more powerful I am —or rather, the more powerful we are as community—in helping multitudes of others. Only the family of communities in Christ can effectively accomplish Christ's mission of healing all human relationships and reconciling all mankind in universal brotherhood.

If we start with what we are, and with what we have, and do what we can, fulfilling our basic community responsibilities in love, we will soon discover that we can do infinitely more than we ever dreamed possible. Our power to love, and to transform the world about us, will increase tremendously precisely when we fulfill our basic baptismal responsibility to give ourselves as true brothers and sisters to all those for whom Christ died, and thus form effective covenant community with others. This is the precise rationale of the Lord in presently raising up charismatic covenant communities all over the world.

God will not save the world through a handful of isolated saints living a stupendously heroic holiness, but through a multitude of ordinary Christians who are seriously carrying on the Lord's own ministry of love and reconciliation in everyday human relationships. For salvation consists precisely in this healing of relationships among the members of mankind, bringing them together into communion with God their Father in a brotherhood of true covenant love.

Each Christian, each family, each group, each community in the Church fulfills its share in the Lord's own mission of salvation only to the extent that it helps build up the body of Christ as a community of communities, in which people love one another in a practical way, as true brothers and sisters who have committed their very persons to one another.

Start with what you have? No, start with what you *are*. Only if our very persons are committed to one another in fraternal love (and this is of the essence of Christian community), can there be salvation of the world in the universal brotherhood of all mankind.

Social Action as Community Task

From what we have been saying, it should be evident that building community, bringing about deep fraternal relationships, accepting full responsibility for one another, sharing all that we are and all that we have with our brothers and sisters in the Lord, is also the fundamental element in all organized social action in the Church, and is indeed the fundamental element in evangelization itself.

Social apostolates will fall short of their Christian purposes if they are not first of all works of building true Christian community. Such apostolates should be but an organic development of the fundamental life of the Christian community which sponsors them. More fundamental than the restructuring of economic, political and social life is the healing of people themselves in their basic human relationships, getting to the very roots of the evils in our human structures by striking at the sin which divides people and sets them against one another, and organizes them for selfish goals so that one group profits at the expense of another. The world cannot be restructured in justice and love unless people are healed of sins and resentment in their very hearts.

Such healing can take place completely only in loving community. The Christian community receives battered, unloved people into its midst and heals them, remaking them in the Holy Spirit by the power of community love.

Therefore we must strive first of all to build true community in the Lord, and at the same time not leave undone the work of restructuring economic, political and social life according to God's will. Many Christians who have been attempting to promote works of social justice through purely human, temporal and political means have come to see, through experience, the truth of what we have been saying. They are beginning to realize that their chief efforts should be directed toward building communities of people with deep personal concern for one another, people who share in fraternal love both what they are and what they have, and yet do not leave undone the work of complete economic, political, and social reform in justice and love.

Charismatic communities have often been censured for neglecting the organized social apostolate. This is an unjust censure, because these communities are carrying on in a beautiful way that more fundamental work of healing people in their human relationships, and building the kind of community which alone can heal the world.

The building of true Christian community goes to the deepest roots of the world's problems: the alienation, divisions, disintegration of basic human relationships. All this disintegration springs from sin, which separates men from one another through selfishness, greed, manipulation of one another for one's own profit or pleasure. Through the healing of human relationships and the building of community, poverty, hunger and oppression are struck in their very roots, and not simply in their superstructure. Only communities of communities will be powerful enough to change the world's structures according to the will of Christ.

The fundamental Christian apostolate, then, is building community: communities of worship, communities of covenant love. Promoting such communities of worship and love is, according to Vatican II, the basic role of priest and bishop; for Christian community is necessarily built around the Eucharist, which is both source and fullness of community in the Lord.[1]

Evangelization as Community Task

We said that building community is even more basic than evangelization; or perhaps we should say that the living of community is the basic form of evangelization. All evangelization springs from community, and community is necessary for the continuation of the Christian mission of evangelization.

The Acts of the Apostles shows that the first effect of the outpouring of the Holy Spirit at Pentecost was not the immediate departure of the apostles to preach to the whole world, but the formation of Christian community (Acts 2:41-47). This community in turn (8:1-4), and later the community at Antioch (13:1-3), sent out missionaries in due time to the rest of the world. All apostolic mission is rooted in community.

The very life of the community is the primary and most effective apostolic witness. In his prayer to the Father, Jesus makes it clear that the truth of the gospel can be made manifest only in community love. "Father, that they

---

1. See Vatican II, *Decree on the Life and Ministry of Priests* (6). Also, Hinnebusch, "The Priest and Christian Community," *The Priest,* Feb. 1972, p. 17f.

may be one even as we are one, I in them and you in me, that they may become perfectly one, so that the world may know that you have sent me, and have loved them even as you have loved me" (Jn 17:22-23).

The gospel or good news is the fact of God's love which has sent his Son to make us all one in this love. Thus the greatest witness to the truth of the gospel is Christians' love for one another. Their love is the living gospel. This is verified in Acts, where we are told that the community life and love drew multitudes to the community (Acts 2:47).

Since community love is the good news, the best evangelization is community love. When this gospel is seen in lives, it draws others into the community, which is itself the good news of God's full communion with those for whom the Lord died.

A charismatic community witnesses to Christ by its very existence as a community of love. Its public prayer meeting, manifesting this community love, is a call to conversion from sinful self-centeredness and alienation to community in the Lord.

Chapter 7

Why a Covenant Commitment?

The baptismal responsibility to build community is best fulfilled when the people involved make an explicit covenant to work together. For our baptismal commitments cannot be fulfilled unless we grasp what they are, and explicitly commit ourselves to fulfilling them. Once we grasp that Baptism is a commitment to fraternal community with others, then we must commit ourselves not only to the Lord, but to all the people with whom we are called to build community.

The new covenant in the blood of Christ to which we commit ourselves in Baptism is expressed in the New Testament in general terms. It is our responsibility to find the specific concrete way in which we are to embody it in our lives in our times and circumstances. Our commitment to Christ and to Christian community must be implemented in a concrete, down-to-earth, effective way of living community with "here and now" persons. We must make an explicit covenant with these persons whom God has brought into our lives and with whom we have the responsibility to live and work in a Christian way. To these persons we must give ourselves in fraternal love, accepting full responsibility for one another.

Certainly bishops and priests, responsible for leading the people in living their Baptism, have the responsibility to lead their people in forming true fraternal community. Only in such community can the people adequately fulfill all their other Christian responsibilities.

A vague and ineffective will to community is not enough. Viable community requires a commitment with others to a stable, living, organic, growing, adaptable body —the body of Christ incarnate in our community.

In the days when Christian community was a little easier to achieve because it had healthy natural communities to begin with, perhaps it was sufficient that the covenant to live as Christian community be implicit. People did not talk much about community, they lived it by the grace of God, transforming in Christ the already existing natural elements of community, which, though troubled by sin, were already more or less cohesive. But under contemporary conditions, in which natural community in loving relationships has all but disappeared in our culture, an explicit covenant to work for community is necessary.

Such a covenant community, implementing our baptismal covenant with Christ, requires a clear commitment to an acknowledged pattern of community relationships. The pattern includes leadership, submission, cooperation, various responsibilities and services to be rendered. The community has to be a living body, an organism with a variety of organs fulfilling various functions or services, all of which must work together for the good of the whole. In Christian community, each of these functions or works is a charism, a grace from the Holy Spirit for building up the body of Christ.

All these charismatic graces or functions in the community are rooted in Christian Baptism and Confirmation. Each Christian has the responsibility to find and fulfill the particular charism or role in the community to which the Lord is calling him and to which the Holy Spirit is leading him.

Only in viable communities effectively putting to work the covenant grace of Baptism, and all the charismatic graces stemming from Baptism, can Christians fulfill the responsibilities of subsidiarity. By subsidiarity we mean that each person and each group in the community fulfills its own functions in freedom and responsibility, not expecting higher levels of responsibility, such as bishops and priests, to do what can and ought to be done on the level of the laity. Or, to put it in terms of the body of Christ, not expecting the heads of communities to carry out the functions of the members, but each member and each organ of the body doing its part.

The charismatic communities which have sprung up in the Church in the past few years are so called because charismatic gifts such as prophecy, healing, speaking in tongues, and the like, are manifest in them in a striking way. But a far better reason for calling these communities "charismatic" is the fact that in them all the charisms of the laity are coming alive in a remarkable way. People are wholeheartedly assuming the responsibility to carry out the various charismatic services and functions necessary for Christian community. These long-neglected responsibilities are being carried out in fuller cooperation with the charisms of the clergy.

There can be no fullness of community where certain charisms or roles in the community are neglected. Vatican II teaches that every member of the Church has his charisms, his ways of rendering service in building up the body of Christ (*Constitution on the Church* 12). The Council insists that pastors must encourage and direct these charisms to full fruitfulness for the good of the whole body.

Anyone who takes a patient and honest look at a charismatic community will discover, along with the more striking charisms such as prophecy and tongues, a multitude of other charisms which are quietly at work, healing human relationships, bringing people together in unity and love, deepening the experience and understanding of integral Christian life and spirituality. Christian marriage, for example, is once again seen as a charism which entails a multitude of lesser charisms working within the family, and integrating the family into the larger community. We must not extinguish the Spirit who is at work in the multitude of the charisms of the laity (cf 1 Thes 5:12, 19-21).

In calling charismatic communities into being, the Holy Spirit began by stirring up charisms of community prayer, especially praise of the Lord. Then through the charism of prophecy, the Lord spoke explicitly to his people of praise, giving them clear directions for forming community in covenant love. When his people bear his yoke together in community, all pulling evenly in unison, his yoke is sweet and his burden is light (Mt 11:29). In community, the Lord manifests his presence in the midst of his people (Mt 18:20). He draws them more deeply into his love, he invites them to go deeper into the knowledge of himself, which he will give them when they acclaim his presence, listen to his word, are attentive to the inspirations of his Holy Spirit, and build one another up in love (Eph 3:14-19).

When a person has seen in faith that a particular covenant community is his God-given way of embodying his baptismal covenant in a practical way of community life, then in love's free choice he gives himself to the covenant community without reserve. He realizes that he is committing himself not only to the Lord in a special way but to all the members of the community as to true brothers and sisters in the Lord. Responsibility for one another is of the essence of Christian community.

To the extent that such a commitment to the community is a concrete, God-given way of implementing the responsibilities assumed in Baptism, it partakes of the seriousness and binding force of the baptismal covenant.

The Right to Covenant Community

Have Christians a right to associate in charismatic covenant communities? Are they not bringing division into the body of Christ when they set themselves up in what look like communities of those who consider themselves some kind of elite?

If we have the responsibility to build a workable Christian community, then we have a right to do it. If other Christians have a right to band together in religious communities as a way of expressing their participation in the covenant in Christ's blood, so Christians are free to associate with other Christians in other viable ways of living the Christian life fully in community.

They do this rightly, of course, only when they form their community in full openness to the rest of the Christian community, striving to integrate it in every way into the whole body of Christ, accepting the headship of their bishop. Pastors, as builders of community, should work to bring about such covenant communities among their people. All such communities should be rooted in the Eucharistic community, and be fruitful in the fullness of community in the Lord.

We have mentioned that the commitment to a covenant community is a commitment to the Lord and to each of the persons making up the community. It is love's commitment to be and to do for others. It is a commitment also to a definite pattern of relationships. The pattern spells out just how we belong to one another in fraternal love, and guarantees the fulfillment of all functions necessary for the community.

However, the covenant of such a community can be implemented and made effective in daily life only through a variety of lesser agreements concerning various details of the community life together. In keeping with the principle of subsidiarity, these lesser agreements are made, not on the highest level of the community leaders, but on the level of the smaller groups making up the community, such as groups of families called "households."

All these agreements, like the covenant itself, and the general patterns of community, are simply directions for loving in a practical way, with love that is not just words, but deeds of service. The various elements in the agreements should be seen as love's guidelines to the most effective ways of promoting covenant love, unity, healing of human relationships, salvation.

Love's conscience accepts love's responsibility to love in the most effective way. Love, enlightened and inspired by the Holy Spirit, does what love sees needs to be done.

Love's Priorities

But love has priorities in what is to be done, for love always sees limitless possibilities, endless needs to be lovingly cared for. Christian love is universal. A disciple of Jesus excludes no one from his love. However, love shows itself in deeds. It is impossible for me to perform loving deeds on behalf of every single member of mankind, or even on behalf of every needy person within my personal sphere of awareness. Love always does what it sees needs to be done, and yet the needs of others with which my love daily comes face to face are so endlessly multiple that, guided by the Holy Spirit, I must make a choice in what I am going to do for others in love.

In making this choice, I must follow what St. Thomas Aquinas calls the order of charity, which sets priorities concerning how I am to love in concrete works of love. There are two basic principles to be applied in determining whom God has given me to be loved in this effective way.

First, I must love above all those who are closest to me because they are dependent upon me, or I am dependent upon them, in a special way. Thus, I must love first my husband or wife, my parents and children, my teachers or pupils, my brothers or sisters in my religious community, my spiritual guides or those subject to my guidance, my employers or employees, my fellow workers and any others bound to me in close ties, or for whose welfare I am responsible in some special way. Thus, the cells of the human hand cooperate more closely with the other cells in the hand than they do with the cells in the feet; and yet all the cells in the body work together in a higher unity.

The more a community's covenant touches upon these essential priorities, such as marriage covenants of its members, or the deeper obligations of religious profession, the more binding it is. In fact, the covenant is made primarily as an effective aid to the fulfillment of the basic Christian charisms and responsibilities, for only in community can these be fulfilled adequately.

But Christian love cannot possibly be content with doing only the minimum, fulfilling only the most basic responsibilities. Therefore there is a second principle in determining love's priorities. In choosing among the multitudes of needy persons who present themselves for my love's help—for I cannot possibly care for all their needs—my love helps first those whose need is most desperate. The more desperate the need of another, the more urgently love presses me to help.

But even this principle must be applied in harmony with the first principle, which obliges me to love in community those closest to me because of my vocation and because of my specific charisms, my ways of serving in the community of mankind at large. In fact, the more completely I am integrated into Christian community with those closest to me (those whom God has given to me to love in a special way), the more powerful I am, with my community, in helping multitudes of others. Only the family of communities in Christ can effectively accomplish Christ's mission of healing all relationships and reconciling everyone in universal brotherhood.

Part 3

God's Image in Community

Chapter 8

Son: Image of the Father

To live in community, we said, is to be "at home" in a network of loving human relationships. But Christian community is first of all a relationship with God, "the Father from whom every family in heaven and on earth takes its name" (Eph 3:14). Just as the relationship of child with father is fundamental in the family, so the relationship of everyone in the community with God as Father is the indispensable foundation of Christian community. We build community in vain unless we build upon this foundation.

Our relationship with God grows not only in prayer and worship, but also in and through our right relationships with one another. Thus, the child grows in relationship with God first of all through his relationship with his parents. Parents are image and presence of God for him. But parents can be a presence of God to their children only to the extent that they themselves are in a right and mature relationship with God.

What parents are for their children, leaders of communities are for the whole community. Since the relationship of each of us with God is still in process of growth, our relationships with God and with one another must be firmly supported by the relationships of the more mature among us with God. Thus, only when fathers of families and leaders of communities are in right relationship with God can their families and communities be in right relationship with them and with one another.

Therefore we turn again to consider the son-father relationship within the family, for in it we have an image of mankind's basic relationship with God. In it we have also a pattern for relationships with God through relationships with one another.

Image and Likeness of God

Every true father, like that daddy bending over the cradle, speaks to his son not only in words, but his whole person is like a word calling to his son, inviting the response which is imitation. By the example of his life, the father calls forth his own likeness in the child. And through his response to the father, a son becomes ever more perfectly the image of his father.

No doubt reflections like these led the inspired author of Genesis to his insight that man is made in the image and likeness of God. In calling man the image of God, the author is simply stating that man is a son of God. This is manifest from a comparison of Genesis 5:3, "Adam became the father of a son in his own likeness, after his image," with Genesis 1:26, "Let us make man in our image, after our likeness." Just as man procreates sons in his own image, so man, created in God's image, is God's son.

Since loving response is of the essence of sonship, as son and image of God, man is essentially response to God's call of love. He is called to intimate communion with his Father.

To be in God's image, then, means to be God's son, existing in loving communion with the Father.

The Image of the Invisible God

This is verified eminently in Christ. "The beloved Son . . . is the image of the invisible God" (Col 1:13,15). Paul does not say that the Son is one image among many. He says that he is *the* image, the only image of God. One alone is God's image: Jesus Christ our Lord.

How can we reconcile Paul's teaching that Christ alone is image with the statement in Genesis that all men are in the image of God?

Genesis does not say that man *is* the image of God. It says that man is made *according to* God's image: "Let us make man in our image, after our likeness" (Gn 1:26). Only of Christ is it said that he *is* the image. Because of sin, we can be in God's image only when we are created anew in Christ, image of the Creator: "Put on the new man, one who grows in knowledge as he is formed anew in the image of his Creator" (Col 3:10).

All our growth in the image of God comes through personal response to God's word, a word of loving invitation directed personally to the heart of each one. But God's perfect word to us is the Son, the Word. Just as the daddy's whole person is like a word of invitation to which the child responds in imitating him, so we respond to the whole person of Christ the Word, who himself is God's word and image, the visible presence of the invisible God.

Image: Presence of the Unseen God

In biblical language, an image is no mere copy or likeness. It is a presence and manifestation of him whose image it is. When Paul says that the beloved Son is "the image of the invisible God," he means that he is the visible presence of the unseen God. Christ alone is the one who reveals God. "No one has ever seen God; the only Son who is in the bosom of the Father, he has made him known" (Jn 1:18). He is the only one who, of himself, adequately expresses God, and therefore he is the only adequate image or manifestation of God. Only an eternal Son, equal to the Father, can be his full expression. The whole Person of Jesus is the Word of the Father to which we respond, and thus become ourselves images of the Father, in the Son.

The Sinner as Image of God

If only Christ is the image of God, and I can be in the image of God only when I am recreated in Christ, how can man apart from Christ, or existing in sin, be in the image of God? Does sin destroy the image of God in me?

I can solve this problem only when I realize that God's image in me is dynamic, not static. It is something into which I grow ever more fully. The image, as sonship, consists in living relationships of recognition and love, in response to God's loving acceptance of me. This knowledge and love deepen. Even after my Baptism into Christ, my growth toward the fullness of the image is an ongoing process. St. Paul uses a present participle to denote a continuing progression: "You have put on the new nature which is *being renewed* in knowledge according to the image of its creator" (Col 3:10).

The beginning of this continuing process is my creation by God. My very coming into being is a response to the call of God's creative word, and therefore in the first instant of my existence I am response to God's love. As response, I am already somehow in God's image.

But at this inital stage, my creation, I am still only *capacity* for a personal response to God in the freedom of knowledge and love. "The Sacred Scriptures teach that man is created in the image of God, *capable* of knowing his creator and loving him" (Vatican II, *Constitution on the Church in the Modern World* 12).

Only in free personal response is my initial created likeness to God brought to fulfillment. Thus, as image, I am ordered in a personal and dynamic way to God my creator and redeemer. The image of God, even in sinful man apart from Christ, is his capacity to respond to God's personal call to him precisely as person.

The Sinner's Recognition of the Father

Even sin does not destroy God's image as capacity to respond. This capacity remains in me as long as I live on earth. Only if I die in defiant rejection of God is his image in me irrevocably distorted.

Sin is a refusal to be God's son. The call to repentance is a call to acknowledge God again as Father. Jesus presents this in terms of the prodigal son, who is an adolescent or young adult who returns to his father. Only in his return home, once again acknowledging his father, this time in an adult way, does the prodigal become fully son, and fully adult.

Just as the young daddy has great joy in his infant's first sign of recognition of him, so the mature father overflows with joy at the return of his son who had rebelled and gone off on his own. Once again, on a deeper level than before, the returned son acknowledges him as father: "Father, I have sinned against God and against you; I no longer deserve to be called your son" (Lk 15:21).

In going away, he had renounced his father and therefore his sonship. He becomes son again, he is reborn, when his father accepts him again in overflowing love and joy: "Let us eat and celebrate, because this son of mine was dead and has come back to life. He was lost and is found" (Lk 15:23). Only the father's love reaching out again to receive him in love perfects both the fatherhood and the sonship in a renewed relationship of mutual loving response and joyous communion.

Even if a son does not rebel to the extent that he totally rejects his father, he nonetheless usually goes through a stage which ends in a renewed recognition and acceptance of his father. At 15, a young man is amazed at the stupidity of his father. At 20 he is astonished at how much his father has learned in the past five years. The learning, of course, is not just on the part of the son. The father grows up, too!

Manifesting God with Christ

If to be image of God is first of all a direct relationship with God as his son, in consequence it is a manifestation of God to others. "He who sees me sees the Father" (Jn 14:9). When the author of Hebrews says that God's Son is "the splendor of his glory and the image of his substance" (Heb 1:3), he is applying to Christ the words about Wisdom: "She is a pure effusion of the glory of the Almighty, a reflection of eternal light, the flawless mirror of the active power of God, the image of his goodness" (Wis 7:25-26).

If as image I am to be a reflection of God to others, God's image in me has to be full and flawless. The glory of God shines to others from a son of God only to the extent that the son has achieved the fullness of sonship in loving response to the Father. Jesus himself comes to his glory only in responsive obedience. "Although he was a son, he learned obedience through what he suffered, and being made perfect, he became the source of eternal salvation to all who obey him" (Heb 5:8).

I too can be image of God reflecting him to others only to the extent that I myself am son of God in Christ, in the fullness of filial response to my Father.

Thus, to be in the image of Christ is to share not only in his filial relationship with the Father, but also in his mission as revelation of the Father to others. "Let your light so shine before men, that they may see your good works and give glory to your Father who is in heaven" (Mt 5:16).

These good works, as described in what immediately follows in the Sermon on the Mount, are above all works of love for one another as brothers and sisters in Christ (Mt 5:21-42). The supreme proof of this love is love even for enemies. "Love your enemies . . . so that you may be sons of your Father in heaven . . . Be perfect as your heavenly Father is perfect" (5:45, 48).

My full image as God's son shines forth to others as a reflection of God's glory, calling them, too, to respond to God.

Chapter 9

Community: Image and Presence of God

God himself is expressed and manifested in man, his image, because God's own Spirit is in man (Gn 2:7), and therefore man participates in God's own life. Man is fully God's image, however, not simply as an individual son living in filial response to the Father, but as a community of brothers and sisters in the Lord. For man is not alone (Gn 2:18), he is a family. "Male and female he created them, in the divine image he created him" (Gn 1:27).

Not simply the individual person, then, but mankind is in the image of God. Or rather, God's full image is in any segment of mankind which exists as family or community in loving relationship in the Holy Spirit.

This insight, already suggested in Genesis, is verified in the fullness of revelation given to us in the person of Jesus. For in Christ, God's Son, God is revealed as a trinity of Persons. Jesus exists with the Father in a loving relationship in the Holy Spirit. Thus he manifests that God is three Persons existing in the fullness of loving communion with each other. God is community.

That is why God's likeness in human persons is complete only to the extent that they are brothers and sisters in the Lord, sons and daughters of God in loving communion with one another in the Holy Spirit. We are in the fullness of God's image and likeness only as community in the Holy Spirit of the Son.

We say "in the Holy Spirit of the Son," because as God's image man is not merely a copy of God. His personal relationships are not simply patterned after God's relationships. Men are image and presence of God because God's own personal life and relationships are present and manifest in their communion with one another in love. This loving communion is a participation in the Holy Spirit of God, who himself is the bond of love uniting the divine Persons and all who participate in the life of these three.

Man receives this full likeness of God only through his participation in the life of Christ, who alone of himself is "the image of the invisible God" (Col 1:15). He alone, of himself, lives in the fullness of communion with the Father, and we can live in this communion only in Christ.

The whole Christ—Jesus together with his body, the Church—is the community of all who are one in him. Only in this community, the body of Christ, is mankind fully perfected as image of God. This is the baptismal community. "For as many of you as were baptized into Christ have put on Christ. There is neither Jew nor Greek, there is neither slave nor free, there is neither male nor female; for you are all *one* in Christ Jesus" (Gal 3:27).

Continuing Christ's Mission as Image

Christ's mission as image is continued by the Church, God's people who are one body in Christ. In its first words to the world, Vatican II echoes St. Paul's words about "the glory of God shining on the face of Christ" (2 Cor 4:6), and speaks of "the light of Christ shining on the face of the Church" (*Constitution of the Church* 1), drawing all men to respond to God who is manifest in the Church, his image.

Though the image of God shines forth in its perfect fullness only in the fullness of love in his community, it shines forth also in each manifestation of this love by members of the community. The Church carries on its mission as image of God through each manifestation of God's love in its members. Thus God's image shines forth in a fundamental way in the Christian father's love for his children. It shines forth also in the love of husband and wife for each other.

All the ways of imaging God within the community are a sharing in the Church's role as image of God, continuing Christ's own mission as image.

That is one of the reasons why every Christian family is a community affair. By the sacrament of Matrimony, Christ and the Church consecrate the couple and commission them to carry on a function in the body of Christ, a function in which they continue the Church's own mission as image and presence of God's love.

In a similar way, the sacred leaders of the Church, the men consecrated by the sacrament of Holy Orders, are image of Christ precisely as *head* of his Church. In this image, Christ as head is present, working through the ministry of his priests.

Also in the various other roles and ministries carried out in the Christian community, Christ is present and manifest in varying ways and degrees. Through all the works of love in the community, the Church continues the Lord's own work as image and likeness of God.

Christian Marriage: Image and Presence of God

We present here a homily given at a wedding in the days when this book was being written. It is a specific application

of the truths we have been considering. The gospel reading
was from the Lord's prayer at the Last Supper, ending with
the words, "Father, I will that the love with which you love
me may be in them, and I in them" (Jn 17:26).

THE HOMILY

Tony and Kathleen, you have just heard Jesus praying for
you two. He asked that the same love with which the
Father loves him may be in you. Earlier at the Last Supper,
Jesus said to you, "As the Father has loved me, so I have
loved you. . . . As I have loved you, so must you love one
another" (Jn 15:9, 12).

Think of what that means, Kathleen and Tony! Jesus
says that you two must love each other in the same way in
which he loved you. And he has loved you in the same
way in which God his Father loved him. You must love
each other not only in the same way that Jesus loved you.
You must love each other with the very same love with
which he loved you. For your love for each other is God's
own love in you. God's love has been poured out into your
hearts by the Holy Spirit who has been given to you (Rm
5:5).

Just how did Jesus love you? He loved you so much
that he gave his life for you on the cross. That is how you
are to love each other. "Husbands, love your wives just
as Christ loved the Church, and gave himself up for her"
(Eph 5:25). Wives, love your husbands in the same way,
with the Lord's own love and self-sacrifice.

Christ's love is everlasting. Nothing can destroy it. "I
have loved you with an everlasting love" (Jer 31:3). The
bible is always talking about God's steadfast love and faithfulness. That is how God loves his people in his covenant
with them. Tony and Kathleen, since you love each other
with God's own love, your love will be everlasting, forever

steadfast and faithful.

Even if in your human weakness you sometimes hurt each other, your love will still be everlasting, for in love you will ask forgiveness, and in love you will forgive. You will forgive each other as Jesus has forgiven you and has laid down his life for you.

Your love will be steadfast and faithful like God's own love for you, because your marriage covenant is a sharing in the new and eternal covenant which Jesus made in his blood with his Church and with you.

Your covenant with Jesus, his covenant with you, can be lived only in your covenant with each other. Your way of living the covenant with Jesus is by being faithful to your marriage covenant with each other. From this moment on, this moment in which you give yourselves to each other in marriage, your only way of being faithful to your God is by being faithful to each other. Your pure and steadfast love for each other is henceforth your fundamental way of expressing your love for God.

Your faithful love for each other will be your way of showing forth to the world God's own enduring and steadfast love. Your love will be the image of God's love. It will be a sign and presence of God's own love in the world.

Only if you love each other with Christ's own love will your children grow up in God's love. As a sign and presence of God's love, your love will be a source of love causing love in your children. If you love your children with God's own love, when they respond to your love, they will be responding to God himself. You will be image and presence of God to them.

From God's love manifest in you, they will learn to love you, and one another, and all their fellowmen, in God's own love, just as you love each other in God's own love. The love will flow from God's heart through your hearts to them, and in responding to your love they will be responding to God's love, for the same Holy Spirit of love is in you and in them.

Thus your marriage and your undying love for each other will be a fountain of God's own love in the world about you. For by the sacrament of Matrimony your love is consecrated within the love of Jesus for his Church, the love in which he died for all of us. Your mission will be to spread that love; Christ loving in you, the love spreading to your family, and from your family speading out to others.

Thus your home will be a link in the great network of love in which God wishes to unite all mankind, so that all of us will be knit together in love, and God's love will thus fill the world. It is your mission in the world, Tony and Kathleen, to show forth God's own everlasting love in your love for each other, and in your love for the family which God will give you.

And you can love in that way only if you die with Jesus for each other, and for all those whom he will entrust to your love.

Your home will not be the house in which you will live. Your home will be the love in which you receive each other, and all the children whom God will give to you. Your home will be the love with which Jesus loves you, the same love with which the Father loves him and he loves the Father. "Live in my love" (Jn 15:9). Home, for your children, will be the love in which you two are at home with God and with each other.

Christian Fathers as God's Image

In the very nature of man as created according to God's image, the father of every family was meant to be the image of God for his family, so that in responding to the father, head of the family, the family would be responding to God. "He is the image and glory of God," says St. Paul, speaking of man as head of his family (1 Cor 11:7).

But a father can carry on this role adequately only within the community of God's people, and only if he himself is son of God through his submission to Christ and to his representatives within the community.

We can grow humanly and in the Spirit only when we are known and lovingly appreciated by those who love us "in the Spirit" (Gal 3:3). If the children of a family are truly to respond to God in responding to their father, then that father must love them in the Holy Spirit, so that in this love, God the Spirit will be present and manifest to them.

The father himself must be truly son and image of God, "beholding the glory of the Lord, and being changed into his likeness from one degree of glory to another, by the Lord who is the Spirit" (2 Cor 3:18). Only he who beholds the glory of the Lord in faith, and prayer, and obedience is able to reflect God's glory, in turn, to others.

The father himself is still growing in the likeness of the Lord, because he himself is daily responding anew to the Lord and to his word and Spirit mediated to him in the community. Just as his children respond to him as image of the Lord, so he himself responds to others in the community who are image of the Lord to him. These others include not only the ministers of the Church, and any others to whose headship he is subject, but also his peers in the community, especially those with whom he is united in special bonds of friendship in the Lord.

In a special way, the husband responds to his wife, as she does to him, for she is God's image to him as much as he is God's image to her.

But if husband and wife together reflect God to their family (for God's image is perfected in mutual love), they themselves need to respond to God's image presented to them in the friendships in the Spirit which are the Christian community. Just as a child can grow only when he is appreciated and cherished by his parents, so the parents can continue to grow on an adult level only if they themselves are appreciated and cherished by other adults. The community in the Spirit, and groups of friends within this larger community, are "the image and glory of God" (1 Cor 11:7) in a way that a lone individual cannot be.

Therefore the word or image which the father presents to his family in his whole person is formed in him by the Word and Spirit of Christ which are present to him in the community. "The head of every man is Christ" (1 Cor 11:3). Through his responsive obedience to Christ, manifest to him in the community, a father grows in the likeness of Christ, and becomes more and more the image of Christ to his family.

A father (like any Christian) responds to Christ in various ways: to Christ as manifest to him in his own conscience; to Christ as revealed to him in community worship; to Christ with whom he is in direct interior communion in personal prayer; to Christ as reflected to him in various ways by other persons in the community; to Christ as revealed to him in his life situations, in all of which Jesus as Lord is present, working for his loving purposes, inviting the father's response.

If the father lives in communion with God in this loving response, then he will reflect to his family what he is receiving from God. The father, himself loved and appreciated by God, will relay the warmth of God's love to his children, who will respond to their loving father as to God himself; for God's love is mediated to them in the father's listening love, and in his loving appreciation of what God is doing in their hearts.

The cherishing love and appreciation with which the father envelops his family is first of all his appreciation of them as created in God's image, endowed with the capacity for direct communion with God. If he venerates his child as image of God, and bends over it with God's own love in the Spirit, then the child will respond to him in love in the Spirit, for the Spirit already dwells in the child because of Baptism. In due time the child will respond directly to the heavenly Father, whom the earthly father has reflected and echoed to him in love which is a participation in God's own love.

The father's loving appreciation of the children is reverence for the children as a masterpiece of God's love, endowed not simply with human potentialities, but with divine potentialities in the Spirit, a supernatural capacity to respond to God. If the father lives in the Spirit, and lovingly cherishes his child as one in whom the Spirit dwells, the father's loving appreciation of the child will help draw forth from the child's heart all the fruits of the Holy Spirit.

Child and father and mother, of course, will bring forth the full fruits of the Holy Spirit only within the larger community of God's people, for these fruits are sown by the Spirit in community prayer, and especially in the Word and Sacrament of the community liturgy, and are cultivated within the fullness of community life. For the family, we have seen, is completed only through its integration into the larger community. We are all one body, one Spirit in Christ.

A father in God's likeness is not one who forces his authority on his family, but one who, by love, invites their loving response. Yet, in love, he firmly holds before them love's requirements, love's responsibilities. For the Lord himself, our Father, forms his sons by his word which expresses his will. The earthly father who lives in the Spirit and reflects upon God's word, firmly but gently presents this will of God to his family, but always inspired by the warmth of God's own love for them.

"The Brother for Whom Christ Died"

What we have shown in the case of a father imaging God

to his family is true of each Christian in his own milieu. Each one may say with St. Paul, "Imitate me as I also imitate Christ" (1 Cor 11:1). Respond to me, image of Christ, because I am responding to Christ, image of God, just as Christ always responded to his Father. As Christ is the loving Word of the Father to me, I am the loving word of Christ to you. Respond to God in responding to me.

Just as the Father has known us in love and we have acknowledged him in love, so in that same love we acknowledge one another as God's beloved sons. "Receive one another as Christ has loved you, for the glory of God" (Rm 15:7). Every one of us must lovingly recognize and reverently receive everyone else as "the brother for whom Christ died" (1 Cor 8:11).

Each is my brother because each is the Father's son. If my brother for whom Christ died has not yet responded to the Father in loving recognition, and therefore acts neither as God's son nor as my brother, nonetheless I love him as my brother; for as God's image, he has the capacity to respond to love, and thus become God's son and my brother. Only my loving appreciation of him as "the brother for whom Christ died" will draw forth from his heart loving recognition of God as Father and of me as his brother.

Only in fraternal communion with one another is our communion with God verified, deepened, and manifest as authentic. "We know that we have passed out of death into life"—into God's life—"because we love the brothers" (1 Jn 3:14).

Chapter 10

Whose Life Have I Touched?

The Lord is truly risen. The convincing proof of this is his real presence in the midst of his people. The most striking and convincing manifestation of this presence is his people's love for one another. In this love, they too are risen and fully present to one another, as a community of true brothers and sisters. "By this we know that we have passed from death to life: by our loving presence to one another" (cf 1 Jn 3:14).

When he rose from the dead, Jesus touched his disciples and let them touch him. "Touch me, and see that a ghost does not have flesh and bones as I do" (Lk 24:39). The point Jesus was making was not so much that he had a body, but that he was truly present with his disciples and really alive.

Already during his ministry on earth before he died, Jesus physically touched those whom he wished to heal or bless in one way or another. "A leper came to him . . . Jesus, moved with pity, stretched out his hand and touched him" (Mk 1:40). "They were bringing children to him

83

that he might touch them" (10:13). His touch was a striking sign of God's real and abiding presence with his people.

Being touched means having someone enter my life
who knows me intimately and lovingly accepts me, so that
I am completely at home with him. Sometimes in our
"Christian" communities, we live day after day in pleasant-
ness toward those around us, but we never really touch very
deeply even one of the persons to whom we are supposedly
committed.

Entering community really means that we commit ourselves not only to the Lord, but to one another. We promise
one another: "I will not stand by and let you die as a person. I will nourish your life and help you live." For we
can live fully as persons only in communion with one another. We are fully alive only in living relationships in love.
And only as interpersonal communion in love are we
image of God.

Therefore to say that I will not let you die as a person
means that I shall touch your life by my full presence. I
shall be present with you in loving knowledge and appreciation. I shall listen to you attentively and really hear you.
I shall truly understand you in loving openness. I shall
accept you as a wonderful work of God's love.

The Risen Lord's Presence

When Jesus was crucified, his disciples felt his death so
deeply precisely because his life had so deeply touched
theirs. His presence to his little community of disciples
had been so full and intimate that the withdrawal of his
presence in his death produced a void in the depths of their
hearts. But the deepest meaning of his death was that it
brought about his intensified presence to those he loved.
His death was a breakthrough to a new, more wonderful
mode of presence with them than his presence among them
before his death. After his resurrection, he was present not

only as a man dwelling among them. He was present in them as God, and they in him.

By way of the cross Jesus goes to the Father and receives the Holy Spirit, whom he pours out upon his disciples as the fruit of his sacrifice. In the coming of the Holy Spirit, the Lord himself comes to dwell in his people. "I will not leave you orphans; I will come to you. Because I live, you will live also" (Jn 14:18).

Because of this marvelous new presence of the Lord after the resurrection, the disciples never tried to return to "the good old days" of their prepaschal experience of Jesus' presence as a man among men. There was no sadness that those days were gone forever. They now experienced the intense spiritual presence of the Lord in their community, in their individual hearts, and in their presence to one another.

Presence to One Another: Life in the Risen Lord

The fraternal love of those who believe in the Lord, we said, is the most convincing proof that the Lord is risen from the dead and the most striking manifestation of his abiding presence. At the same time, this brotherly love is the unmistakable sign that the Lord's followers have risen with him to new life in the Spirit, and in him are lovingly present to one another. "By this we know that we have passed from death to life, because we love the brothers" (1 Jn 3:14).

Love for one another is a presence to one another in attentive love and knowledge. The Lord himself is truly present in such love, for it is impossible except in the Lord's own Spirit. Indeed, this love is the most important and most necessary of all the ways of entering into the Lord's death. For to be fully present to others in loving attention and appreciation requires that we die to self, thus passing with Christ through death to new life. All this is possible, however, only because the Lord himself touches us by his presence to us.

A Teacher's Witness

A teacher recently wrote me a letter telling about a real death to self that was accomplished in her through her loving presence to one of her pupils, a high school girl who was bitter, mean, resentful and rebellious. By temperament this teacher is warm and outgoing, and to see her loving everyone makes one think that it must be very easy for her. But it is not as easy as it looks. Only the Lord's own love in her is gradually transforming her so that she can love universally, in a healing way. She writes:

> For the first time I am beginning to really see the meaning of our vocation to be Christ's presence: It means to love the *unloved*. Usually I have no trouble whatsoever genuinely loving a person who comes to me. Yet this week one of the girls seemed to be needing my love. I was not at all attracted to her. I did not feel like going out to her. I was almost repelled by her. But after much effort with her over a period of days, she finally poured out her heart to me about her problems. She felt so unloved and unable to go out of herself. She said I was the first person in her whole life who had ever loved her. And do you know what? I found that my original feelings of aversion toward her changed into real joy in her presence—and love! I really felt *the Lord* in me loving her, loving the unloved and creating a person who was *lovable!* I even now see a change in her, from cold defensiveness to a softer, gentler way.

Another letter some months later reported the still greater wonders which love was accomplishing in the girl, making her into a loving person for the first time, so that at last she is really living.

St. Francis's Victory Over Self

We read of a similar incident in the life of St. Francis of Assisi. As a wealthy young man, Francis had always been generous to the poor. His naturally affable temperament made it easy for him to be loving. But there was a limit to his love. There was one type of needy person whom he could not bear to go near: the lepers who abounded in the vicinity.

But one day while he was out riding his horse, Francis saw a repulsive leper in the road before him begging for food. By the power of the crucified Lord's love suddenly working in his heart, Francis completely conquered his usual revulsion. Instead of simply tossing a coin as he would have done in the past, he leaped from his horse and embraced the leper, giving him the love and friendship he needed.

After this death to self and resurrection to new life in the Lord, Francis was overwhelmed with joy, and proceeded on his way singing God's praises as never before. He was alive at last—and so was the leper!

Such examples show that absolutely universal love of others is not possible to human nature by itself. It is possible only to a person who dies with Christ and lives in the Spirit. Even the pagans love those who love them, says Jesus. But to love enemies, and those who are utterly repulsive to us, is the mark of the authentic Christian, the man who lives in the Spirit. If we cannot love in this way, we had better pray to the crucified Lord to release the fullness of the Holy Spirit in our hearts.

Whose Life Have I Touched?

The deepest meaning of the Lord's death was that it effected his intensified presence to those he loved. My deepest way of entering into the death of Jesus is by dying to self and becoming more present, more deeply touching the persons around me. Before his resurrection, the death of Jesus caused an intense void in the life of his disciples. In whose life, of those in community with me, would my life cause an intense void?

If I must answer, "No one's," it is because I have not really touched anyone in the presence and intimacy of love and friendship. Consequently, I have been closed also to the more intimate interior touch of Jesus himself in prayer, because I have not been open to my brothers and sisters in the Lord.

Therefore let us ask our Lord's and one another's forgiveness for not entering into the meaning of his death, for not being present to one another in love. Jesus, forgive us for letting the needy among us starve. Jesus, forgive us for letting the lonely among us die.

Perhaps I will excuse my failure, and explain why I have been frightened to touch others by saying that no one has touched my life. I must not give this as an excuse. I must not let my heart shrink by feeling sorry for myself. I must go out of myself and touch others. I will become lovable only by loving. As St. John of the Cross expressed it, "Where there is no love, put love, and you will find love."

We can put love in the midst of our fellowmen because God's love has been poured into our hearts by the Holy Spirit who has been given to us (Rm 5:5).

By our death to self in self-giving presence to one another, we will know that we have passed from death to life in Christ. In this presence to one another, the Lord himself is present among us.

Chapter 11

Friendship and Community: Image of God as Friend

The total gospel is not contained in the one scene in which Jesus says, "I was hungry and you gave me food" (Mt 25:35). Giving to others is not the sole criterion of gospel living. Community and friendship is a more complete Christian way of living than merely concentrating on helping the needy. My Christian love is defective if I think it consists only in giving things to the needy, but never giving myself to them in friendship, and refusing to enter with them into the mutual dependence of community.

For the person who prides himself on being a cheerful giver, but never humbles himself to receive, is only half a Christian. It is harder to be humble in receiving than to be generous in giving. It is more difficult to let someone wash our feet than to wash the feet of another. Yet both are essential in Christian community.

Matthew's scene describing the Christian as one who *gives,* one who serves Christ himself by serving "the least of his brothers," is complemented by Paul's description of Christians as those who *need* one another, those who know how to *receive* in loving humility. "The eye cannot say to the hand, 'I have no need of you,' nor again the head to the feet, 'I have no need of you' " (1 Cor 12:21). We all need one another, and together we exist in the solidarity of neediness before God.

In fact, Matthew 25:31-46, if we read it correctly, really describes every Christian as one who is poor and needy. Jesus says, "Insofar as you did this to one of the least of these brothers of mine, you did it to me" (Mt 25:40). Jesus has identified himself with the poor and needy, that is, with all of us. "Needy brother of mine" is really the Lord's description of every one of his followers.

Therefore a Christian is one who knows how to receive as well as how to give. He knows how to live in the fullness of loving communion and sharing in which there is both giving and receiving. Christian covenant love is communion in mind and heart, expressed in the mutual sharing of all that we are and have.

Indeed, Christian love is receiving before it is giving. Even while it is giving, it is receiving. The fullness of covenant communion is itself ever being received from God. For a disciple is first of all one who surrenders himself totally to the Lord in faith, in order to receive from the Lord. Believing is receiving. "To as many as received him, by believing in his name, he gave the power to become sons of God" (Jn 1:12).

Not only the individual believer, but the whole Christian community is ever receiving the life-giving Spirit from the risen Lord, even while, in turn, it is giving to "these brothers of mine," the needy ones in whose persons we serve the Lord himself.

The mutual giving and receiving among Christians is the expression of a more profound communion with one another in God. It is the expression of their friendship with God, and with one another in God. God is friendship, for

God is communion in love. He is the loving communion of the three divine Persons. The joy of Christian friendship is the image of God as Friend rejoicing in his friendship with his people.

The Christian community is a network of friendships, of close relationships with one another in Christ. The new covenant in the blood of Christ needs to be expressed not only in the whole Christian assembly celebrating the Eucharist together; it needs to be expressed in a multitude of friendships among Christians in everyday life. The network of friendships is necessary for full participation in the covenant community.

Out of such community and friendship springs the apostolate to the poor and needy in which we pour out our loving aid to them. But we do not limit this love to feeling sorry for the needy and helping them only in a paternalistic way, but not wanting their friendship! Our mission to the poor and to sinners desires above all else to bring them into the fullness of our own communion in the friendship of the three divine Persons.

For this God of ours is not a God who aids his poor and needy creatures in a merely paternalistic way, giving them only their material necessities out of his wealth, but having no personal loving concern or friendship for them. God wants to do infinitely more for us than clothe our nakedness, feed our hungry bodies, and provide a beautiful material world for us. He wants to have the joy of full communion with us. He wants us to have the joy of full friendship with him. He is nothing less than a Father and Friend who wills to bring us all into full communion in his own life and joy.

As image of God, then, friendship and community reveal the true nature of God. They show that God is not simply the one who provides for our temporal necessities, such as sunshine and rain and crops in due season, but is a trinity of Persons who bring us into communion in their own inner life, and into the joy of their own intimate relationships.

That is why we are not really Christian if all we do is feed the hungry and clothe the naked and shelter the homeless in a condescending, paternalistic way, but wanting no friendship or community with the ones we help. The truly Christian social apostolate, and concern for justice to the poor, springs from the fullness of covenant love and community, and from the fullness of communion with God in prayer, and seeks to bring the needy ones into the brotherly love and friendship which is community, and thus into the fullness of communion with God.

Therefore Christians who serve in the works of charity manifest among themselves this communion with God in love, this joy of friendship, this brotherhood of God's own children, for only thus do they fulfill their mission as image of God to their needy fellowmen, manifesting the God who rejoices in his friends.

The apostolate of bringing God's friendship to all is never concerned exclusively with aiding the needy, but "rejoices with those who rejoice" as much as it "weeps with those who weep" (Rm 12:15). Weeping with those who weep, that is, coming to the relief of their neediness, is effective to the extent that it springs from the joy of community in the Holy Spirit. For only joy can effectively expel sorrow. In the warmth of friendship in the Lord, friends learn to bring warmth and love more effectively to others. They do this completely only by bringing the others into the community and its joy.

Only in the midst of friendship can human relationships be healed. Those who have never been loved, and have therefore grown up in bitterness and resentment, are healed, and learn to love, only within friendship and community. This healing of human relationships, and drawing forth healing love from hurt hearts, is a more basic and more lasting apostolate than one which merely scratches the surface of human misery by giving only material relief to the needy, and which stands aloof from those to whom the material help is given.

The joy of friendship and community is accompanied by a deep consciousness of our mutual neediness, cared for by God's love which is present to us in each other. It is accompanied by a sense of solidarity with all our fellow-men in total neediness before God, receiving everything from his love, receiving it together, receiving it through one another, receiving it in solidarity with the whole Christian community.

Above all, in community with one another we are ever receiving God's gift of covenant love in the Holy Spirit, without which man cannot live.

Chapter 12

Image of God in the Use of Creation

Our fraternal love for all the brothers for whom Christ died is not mere sentiment or just words. It has to be expressed in a variety of practical ways. It has to be made incarnate, as it were, embodied in the ways we serve one another. We have to be the image of God's love in the way we use his creation for the benefit of our fellowmen.

All creation is the gift of God's love. The Lord entrusted it all to man, his image and likeness, that man might develop and use it for the purposes of love.

But even while he uses and develops creation, man contemplates it, and rejoices in it as a sign and manifestation of God who is love.

Created nature does not fully manifest God's love, however, until man rightly uses and develops it in love. Man's selfish abuse of nature obscures God's love which should be manifest in it. Only by using creation in love is man image of God as ruler of creation. For man's love, developing and using God's gifts in order to serve his fellowmen, is the sign and expression of God's own providence, and of God's love expressed in that providence. God's own love is operative and manifest in man's loving providence for his fellowmen. Thus, as image of God, man is more than sign. He is presence of God's own cherishing love.

This is beautifully illustrated in St. Joseph, father of the Holy Family at Nazareth. We sing of him in the preface of the Mass for his feast: "With a husband's love he cherished Mary, the virgin mother of God. With fatherly care, he watched over Jesus your Son, conceived by the power of the Holy Spirit." Joseph is true image of God's fatherly providence. He is not just its likeness; his love for Mary and Jesus is the very presence and reality of the Father's love and providence for them. God's loving care was operative in Joseph's loving care.

In his work as carpenter, moreover, Joseph's fatherly providence and God's was extended to all who benefited from this work.

The Economic Order as Image of God's Love

Thus, like Joseph, a man is image of God and his providence not only in lovingly providing for his wife and children, but in using his skills and his labor in serving his fellowmen in love. God's loving presence will be everywhere manifest in the human and technological world only when men learn to use their knowledge and their trades, their science and their technology, their labor and their commerce, to serve their fellowmen in love. If their work and trade are characterized by cheating and manipulation of their fellowmen, God's love and presence are obscured, and men no longer know him as Father.

The whole economic order must mirror God's love. Only when mankind is a community of love will this be fully so. In the whole world of labor and business, in all relationships of employer and employee, of buyer and seller, the universal brotherhood of men must be made operative and manifest, otherwise the heavenly Father will be the unknown God. The business world has to be a fraternal community; otherwise it is unchristian. Everyone who makes or trades with the goods produced from God's creation through human work must consider himself a good steward of God's gifts of love, producing and using and distributing these gifts only in justice and fraternal love.

Anyone who provides in any way for the needs of his fellowmen, then, is truly image of God and his loving providence, if he does all this in love. In providing for his family, for example, a father must take care that he never does this in an impersonal way. It is not enough for him to "bring home the bacon" and toss it on the table. He must care for the material and spiritual needs of his family in a context of attentive, listening love, a love which is concerned for his wife and family as persons, who can develop as persons only in deep relationships of love and mutual concern. He is not image of God, if he provides only material abundance for his family. He is image and presence of the heavenly Father only if he provides all things in attentive love.

Too many hardworking fathers have learned this the hard way. They have given their children material goods and comforts in great abundance, and yet have produced only rebellious, alienated teenagers who have run away from home to seek love and community elsewhere. It is not enough to provide an abundance of material goods for one's family. What is needed above all is "the bread of life," loving words uttered in loving concern, loving attention to the human need for love and presence.

From all this we can see that man is image of God not primarily because he has dominion over the earth (Gn 1:27-28) and can develop riches for himself out of God's creation. He is image of God first of all because he was created for communion in love, communion with God as son of God, communion with his family as their father, communion with all his fellowmen as their brother. He develops the earth and its riches only to express this loving communion by providing for those whom God has given him to love all that they need. They need first of all loving communion. Christians express their communion in mind and heart by joyously sharing with one another all the gifts of God's love which they have developed from his creation.

This is the pattern for the whole human family. The riches of the earth will be seen as the gift of God's love, and God will be manifest everywhere as Father, only when by our labors and commerce we provide these things for one another in a fullness of fraternal love. The whole economic and political order, we said, must mirror God's love. Only when mankind is a community of love will this be fully so. Our baptismal covenant with Christ gives us the responsibility to see to it that it will be so. We must enter into covenants of love to make it so.

We must begin with real communities where our communion in mind and heart is fully expressed in effective community of goods. This is happening in reality in many charismatic communities.

At the Lord's final coming, our judgment will be based precisely upon what we have done, or have failed to do, in carrying out this work of universal love.

Community of Possessions

Because everything belongs to God and to Christ, no individual may use what he possesses without taking into consideration the needs of his fellowmen. Because Christians have one heart and one soul in Christ, they are truly brothers, and consequently share all that they have. The Christian who has possessions has the mission to love others in the name of God by passing on God's blessing to them.

This sharing is the indispensable sign of God's love in

which we are all brothers. It is a free and voluntary sharing in love. "The company of those who believed were of one heart and soul, and no one said that any of the things which he possessed was his own, but they had everything in common. . . . There was not a needy person among them, for as many as were possessors of lands or houses sold them, and brought the proceeds of what was sold and laid it at the apostles' feet; and distribution was made to each as any had need" (Acts 4:32-35).

The community of goods, resulting from our union in heart and soul, can be realized in different ways. It can be accomplished in the most literal way possible, where all goods become collective property, administered to each according to his need. But it can be accomplished also, and perhaps better, where each one is so full of God's love that he joyfully, willingly, puts himself, his talents, his work, his goods, his money at the service of whoever is in need. Each person is fully responsible before God for all that has been entrusted to him, and in love he fulfills this responsibility by giving all that he is, and all that he has, to the service of his fellowmen.

All that we are and have, and all that we produce by our work and by our intelligence, belongs ultimately to Christ, to whom our very being belongs. We are only stewards of our heavenly Father's creation, which belongs to all his children, all mankind, and is to be administered lovingly in justice to all. No one may use what he possesses without considering the needs of others. In using what he has, each must care first of all for those for whose lives he is directly responsible, such as his wife and children, and those who are dependent upon him in other ways. Since all things are to be used only in expressing love, each must follow the order of charity which we have indicated in Chapter Seven.

The order of charity is the indispensable norm in using

not only material goods, but also in using whatever talents or gifts of mind or body we have, whatever skills or abilities God has bestowed upon us, whatever graces or charisms he has poured out upon us. God's love and providence for all mankind must be expressed in our use of all his gifts.

This is not an impossible ideal. Christ died to make it possible, and we have the responsibility to put it into effect by the power of his Spirit.

Jesus: Presence of God's Indestructible Love

St. Joseph's love for Mary and Jesus, and his loving service of his fellow citizens as a carpenter, we said, was the tangible reality of God's own love for them. When Jesus, in turn, early in his preaching career, comes to his native town, Nazareth, to proclaim the good news, he comes to all his fellow citizens in the role Joseph had fulfilled before him. He comes as visible presence of God's cherishing love.

> He came to Nazareth where he had been reared, and entering the synagogue on the sabbath . . . the book of Isaiah was handed him. He unrolled the scroll and found the passage where it was written: "The Spirit of the Lord is upon me . . . He has sent me to bring glad tidings to the poor" (Lk 4:16-19).

Jesus comes as image of God, providing for poor and needy mankind, providing above all for man's supreme need, his need for God's own life-giving Spirit. Man is fully in the image of God only when he is in communion with God in the Spirit of his Son.

St. Luke's version of that visit of Jesus to his hometown is really a composite picture piecing together several visits home. On the first visit, when he reads from Isaiah, the people receive him with joy, and marvel at his words of grace (Lk 4:22). But on a later visit they reject him, despising him, saying, "Is not this Joseph's son?" (4:22). A mere carpenter!

How can we explain this complete about-face from acceptance to rejection? First, it seems that they were guilty of selfish possessiveness when they first accepted him. They were using God's gifts in a selfish way. They wanted to keep Jesus for themselves so that they could proudly bask in his glory.

But they became envious when Jesus seemed to be working more miracles elsewhere than in his hometown (4:23). He seemed to be giving more glory to Capernaum than to them! So they turned against him and tried to kill him (4:29). They reject him who is the tangible presence of God's own love, the giver of God's life-giving Spirit.

He came, ready to pour out his own Spirit and love into our hearts: "The Spirit of the Lord is upon me . . . to preach good news to the poor!" (4:18). But we rejected him! "He came unto his own, and his own received him not" (Jn 1:11).

This rejection did not cause him to withdraw his presence and his love. God's love does not offer itself only once, and then withdraw when it is rejected. Jesus stayed on, though they beat and scourged and killed him. Still he stayed on, but now in his risen body. For God's love is indestructible. No attack upon it can destroy it. Jesus is forever the image, the presence and manifestation of God's love.

He is forever the Crucified One, the one whose love for us can never be destroyed by our attacks upon him. Because his hands are nailed down to the cross, he cannot strike back at us when we attack him. Because his feet are nailed to the cross, he cannot back away when we strike him. In the very instant that our sins thrust a lance into his heart, he pours out from it blood and water, symbol of the life in the Spirit poured out upon us in Baptism and the Eucharist. Even in his body of glory, he still bears the marks of the wounds, showing them to us as he showed them to the apostle Thomas. He is forever the image and presence of God's indestructible love for us.

That is why St. Paul comes preaching Christ crucified. He proclaims the same message which Jesus brought to Nazareth. "The Spirit of the Lord is upon me," said Jesus at Nazareth. "I came in the convincing power of the Spirit," says Paul to the Corinthians (1 Cor 2:4). "I proclaimed God's testimony," I told only of his indestructible love manifest and given in the Crucified One, "I spoke of nothing among you but of Jesus Christ and him crucified" (2:1-2). Jesus is the one who gives "the convincing power of the Spirit," so that your faith "rests on the power of God" (2:4-5).

The Church, exemplified by St. Paul, continues the Lord's own mission of indestructible love.

Chapter 13

Response to the Father in Christ

Son is loving response to father. The Christian as son of God is in the image and likeness of Christ's filial response to the Father. We who had departed from God in the disobedience of sin can return to him only in the loving obedience of Jesus his Son.

The word "obedience" is often resented by a person who has never had a listening father. Such a one finds it hard to look upon God as a loving Father, and bristles in resentment at the mention of God's will. He thinks of obedience only as forced submission to another's will, or as a servile capitulation in fear and cowardice. Since his own father has not been a loving listener, he thinks that every father, and therefore God, is one who arbitrarily imposes his will upon others.

But such is not the Father revealed in Jesus, Son and Image of God.

Jesus always listened to his Father's love, because the Father always listened in love to him. Jesus deeply experienced this love: "As the Father has loved me, so have I loved you" (Jn 15:9). Jesus was attentive to this love, and responded to it: "For this reason the Father loves me, because I lay down my life . . . I do as the Father has commanded me, so that the world may know that I love the Father" (Jn 10:17; 14:31). The relationship of Jesus and his Father is mutual love and response. Obedience is filial love.

The Father had listened in love to needy mankind, and in love had asked his Son's love to carry out a mission of loving redemption. His Son's entire human life was a loving response in obedience to the Father's love for all mankind. "On coming into the world he said, 'I have come to do your will, O God' " (Heb 10:5).

The Son's filial response to the Father was never revoked, but was renewed and deepened in every conscious action of his life. His bread of life was always the word of the Father: "My food is to do the will of him who sent me, that I may accomplish his work. For not on bread alone does man live, but on every word that comes from God's mouth" (Jn 4:34; Mt 4:4).

Christ's filial response is continued in his agony: "Abba, Father, all things are possible for you; remove this cup from me; yet not what I will, but what you will" (Mt 14:36). It is perfected in the instant of his death: "Father, into your hands I commend my spirit" (Lk 14:36).

Fully open to his Father's invitations, Jesus thoroughly listened to and obeyed his Father's love. That is why he came to his glory. "He became obedient unto death . . . Therefore God highly exalted him" (Phil 2:8ff).

When we say "Yes" to an invitation of God's love, we open ourselves to a beautiful experience, to an ever-fuller experience of the Lord and his love. God's word is always a word of love. His will is always an invitation of love. Obedience is listening to love. In our responding to his word and love, he fills us with his love and presence.

If bad earthly fathers have obscured the nature of God as Father, Jesus has again clearly revealed God as Father. If my earthly father has failed to listen to me lovingly, and has thus failed to be an image of the loving God for me, then I can discover the God of love in someone else who has loved me and listened to my heart; I can discover him best in a loving community.

If I have had a loving, listening father, I already experience obedience and sonship as a response to love. This is true of my submission to anyone who has authority in the home or in the community. The love to which I listen in obedience has first listened to me, and therefore asks me to do only what love has discerned as being in my best interests. Such is God's love, present and imaged to me in loving authority. Such love invites, rather than commands.

But even when it has to command what I resist, or has to discipline or coerce me, it is still indestructible love, and in the long run it will win my love and dispel my resentment. God my Father is indestructible love, and nothing that I can do can destroy his love for me.

I can believe in a God who is love more easily because I have had an earthly father who has listened to me in love. Parents should love their children so completely and forgivingly that they can easily believe in the God who loves and forgives. "Home" is such a fullness of love and forgiveness that sons and daughters cannot help but be drawn by the beauty of God's love for them. Because the father of the family, like God himself, is indestructible love, a son has no fear in returning to his father if he sins against family love. The father of the prodigal son in Christ's parable is not an impossible dream, it is a Christian reality. God is that way, and so he expects earthly fathers to be that way, images of his own undying love.

Such a father inspires no resentment or rebellion in his sons, unless perhaps he becomes too protective, too helpful, too possessive at those times when the child or youth needs to be independent and to experience his growing powers.

The little child, for example, comes to experience himself as a distinctive person only through being able to do things on his own, mastering his little environment. He wants to and has to do these things without interference from his elders, and will resent excessive guidance and protectiveness. Yet he wants to know and has to know that the father's love is watching and waiting in the background, and is rejoicing in the son's growth.

When a father listens and watches in love, a child responds in love. And his obedience to guidance is not characterized by resentment; nor will the mention of God's will, and the necessity of following it, cause resentment in him.

Relationships Healed in Community Love

If we have spent so much time on what home and fatherhood should be, we have done so because lack of loving homes has produced such devastating effects on modern society. We have done so because we wish to bring out the role of loving community in receiving and healing those who have not had loving homes.

Those who have not received love in their families can find it at last in God's own love poured out to them in a truly Christian community. The community receives the unloved and the unloving, and restores their power to love. It heals the broken relationships between husbands and wives, parents and children, the younger generations and the older ones. In the midst of loving community, loving fathers and mothers and loving families come into being.

This has proved to be one of the most effective apostolates of charismatic communities: the healing of human relationships, the healing of hearts hitherto unable to love because they have been unloved, by pouring out love to them in a community of people who truly do love.

Many a home has failed to be a home, a place of love,

not entirely through the fault of the parents who have failed to love. Their very failure to love has sometimes been due to the fact that they were too isolated from true community of love, and did not receive the community help they needed. No family is sufficient to itself. On its own, it cannot even provide all the love it needs to provide.

For example, a family may be helpless to provide all the human warmth and loving concern it should because it is so poor that father and mother are both forced to work so hard and so long each day that they have no time or energy for showing love and concern for each other or for their children. Loving fellowship requires leisure time, and also security from undue worry about life's material necessities. No home should be destitute. The Christian community should be so organized in love that it can be said in truth, "There was not a needy person among them" (Acts 5:34). Many families have failed to be homes, places of love, precisely because they had to go it alone, without the support of a community of love.

Even when they did not have to go it alone because of poverty, they tried to do it alone for other reasons. They were so intent on the pursuit of earthly possessions or ambitions, for example, that they had no time left for human relationships. There are mothers who take jobs so that they can earn money to provide all the luxuries and comforts they crave, or fathers who get involved in the competitive business world, claiming that they do so only so that they can provide their families with fine things. But just in the effort to maintain a beautiful home, or rather, a lovely well-furnished house, they have no true home, no loving human relationships, because they have exhausted their energies in the pursuit of material comforts. They have perverted their values.

Their children, though they have been provided richly with material comforts, grow up resentful and restless because they have been shortchanged on loving appreciation as persons who can grow rightly only in loving communion.

Community love, in charismatic communities, receives people who are deeply hurting because they have never had real homes, and heals them. Teenagers, for example, who have been alienated from their parents have been taken into other loving homes so that their hurts can be healed.

At the same time, provision needs to be made for the healing of their parents. The parents need to be shown that they have not necessarily been total failures. The fault was not necessarily entirely their own, but some of the blame rests on all of us for our failure to provide loving communities as the matrix of loving homes. Community love is the indispensable support of family love.

Perhaps some of the false values of our families, and their excessive concern for material comforts, are due to the fact that we have had too little experience of the true values, such as genuine fraternal love in the community of God's people. It is the mission of the Christian community to provide this loving fellowship in the Lord, this taste of the divine love for which we were created. Perhaps we have not been living in communion with God, because we have not been living in communion with one another. We fill up the great void in our hearts by the pursuit of material comforts, and are swallowed up in the vicious vortex.

Loving community is the only remedy, a community love which provides many services to fulfill each other's needs, but especially a love which knows how to find joy in loving fellowship, having a good time together in leisure, enjoying being with those we love. A Christian community not only prays together, but also plays together.

Many religious communities have collapsed because they did not play together. They had little time or concern for being together in love, enjoying one another's company.

Charismatic communities are aware of the need for "fellow-shipping," having a good time together in the presence of the Lord, singing psalms and hymns and spiritual songs together, singing not only to praise God with words and music, but singing also in the joy of being together as God's family living in his presence. In facing the tasks and difficulties of life, "rejoicing in the Lord is our strength" (Neh 8:10). The Lord's yoke, the yoke of loving self-sacrifice for one another in community, is sweet, whereas the yoke which we have to carry alone in a competitive world is bitter.

"Though Father and Mother Forsake Me"

If I have never experienced a true home, if I have grown up unloved and unloving, I must beware of making excuses of my own sinfulness and rebellion by saying, "I came from a broken home, from an unloving family." For no doubt I have compounded the sinfulness of my parents and family by sinning against them in return by my spiteful resentment.

But though I may not have known a loving father or mother, it is still possible for me to know God as a loving Father. Through my very experience of an unloving father and of a home which was not a home, I know by contrast what home and loving parents should be. I know it, because my whole being longs for it; and because I have not experienced it, I know all the more poignantly what love is when I see it in others.

Thus I am all the more ready to respond to it when I see it in Christian community. Through my negative experience of lack of love, I am all the more open to God's love when he calls himself my Father. I know what "father" is through what I did not experience from my earthly father or mother, because my whole being was made by God to be a response to love.

Some of the most ardent lovers of God, the most deeply responsive to his love, have been precisely the poorest of the poor, that is, those who had been so starved for human love, that when they found God's love given to them in community, they were all the more profoundly appreciative of it, and therefore responded to the Lord in an amazing wholeheartedness. Those who have been the emptiest are often the ones with the deepest capacity to be filled by the Lord, for they are not cluttered up with false loves and wrong values.

In experiencing my deepest nature, then, empty though I may be of love, I experience that I was made for love, and in my very nature I somehow know what alone can fill that emptiness. My whole nature is an emptiness crying out to be filled with God my Father.

Therefore I must stop my self-pity and my resentment of my bad parents, and believe when I am told that God is Father. I must not think of God as the type of father whom perhaps I have experienced, one who only barks out arbitrary commands and pays attention to me only to punish me. I must think of God as the kind of father for whom my whole being cries out. God who has made me for love will be Love for me. God will still be my Father though all others fail me. "Though father and mother forsake me, the Lord will receive me" (Ps 27:10).

My nature, then, cries out for God my Father, because God has made my nature as capacity to respond to his love and call. I must ratify this cry of my deepest being by joyfully and willingly accepting God's love, crying out to him in the Holy Spirit, "Abba, Father!" Thus I will be in the likeness of Christ's own response to the Father. Jesus continued to love God as Father though the whole world turned against him and crucified him, and in that same love continued to love all his brothers, for whom he died. Never again after that am I justified in sinning against those who have sinned against me.

Part 4

Appreciation: Key to Community

Chapter 14

Appreciation as Fullness of Love

Community in its fullness is where everyone is at home in the brotherly appreciation he receives from others. Loving appreciation of one another is a key element in all genuine community life.

Appreciation is a fullness and overflowing of love. This is evident from a comparison of "need love" with "appreciative love." In need love, I love another chiefly because he is the source of what I need. I love him for what he has to offer me, for what he does for me or gives to me. My love for my father, for example, begins with need love.

But in appreciative love, I love another for what he is in himself, rather than for what he does for me. In the fullness of appreciative love for another, I stand in awe before the mystery of his being. I overflow with admiration and reverence for him, I am enraptured by the beauty and wonders I see in him, and I rejoice that he is what he is. This is a mature kind of love, a going out to others, rejoicing in them for what they are in themselves rather than in what they do for me. Love in its fullness is appreciation.

Thus, my relationship with my father has reached a fullness when I respond to his loving appreciation of me with my loving appreciation of him. Our acceptance of each other in appreciative love is an integral element of our loving communion with each other as persons.

Such mutual appreciation in loving communion is the fullness of every truly human relationship. Every human being deserves such appreciation. For Christian love recognizes, accepts, and rejoices in the profound human and divine worth of every person redeemed by Jesus. To appreciate another in love is to hold him dear and to rejoice that he is what he is, child of God and brother of Christ.

In saying that appreciation is a key value in community, we mean far more than appreciation of what people do for us, or gratitude for the services they render us. We mean appreciation of them as persons, and joy in what they are. The values we love in this appreciation are not the things we possess together or the things we do for one another, but the highest of all human values, the very persons in whom we rejoice. The joy of loving communion with others is the highest of all values, the deepest of all joys.

What we are for one another is inexpressibly more precious than what we do for each other. What my daddy *is* is more precious than what he gives me. What my wife *is* is more precious to me than what she does for me. What God *is* for me is more precious than all that he gives and does in the entire universe.

I come to my appreciation of you as a person, of course, partly through what you do for me. I grow to appreciative love of you through need love for you, since the admirable person you are is manifest in part through the loving services you render me. But what you are in yourself, and your wonderful qualities as a person, far surpass in worth anything you could ever do for me. My love for you therefore appreciates you above all for what you are, and only secondarily for the services you render me. I love you and admire you and rejoice in you and even praise you, but only secondarily thank you for what you do for me.

The truth of this is manifest already in a child's love for his father. He loves his daddy, the person, far more than he loves all that his daddy gives him. This is true also of a man's love for his wife. She does not care too much if he rarely says "Thank you" for the great many services she renders him, if it is quite obvious in his whole bearing toward her that he deeply loves and appreciates her as the wonderful person she is. He will acknowledge what she does for him as the overflowing of her own beautiful self, and any words of thanksgiving to her will be but the expression of joy in her as a person.

Degeneration of Need Love

Without a deep appreciation of persons, my love for others can deteriorate into a degenerate form of need love, which uses others sheerly for my own advantage and manipulates them for my purposes. In human relationships we receive as well as give, and we always need one another. But my love in accepting from you whatever you do for me is saved from selfish grasping, and from manipulating you, only if I have a deep loving reverence for you as a person. My need love for you will remain good and healthy only within the context of strong appreciative love for you.

I do not need to be served by you in order to love and appreciate you. The more mature I am in loving, the less I am characterized by the need love which looks to you or to others to fulfill my wants, and the more I love with a love which rejoices in you and others sheerly because you are persons, beautiful children of God. It is love like this which brings out the best in you, so that you grow in lovableness in response to my love.

Though I will always need to receive from others, as I mature in love I will be loving far more persons than are actually benefiting me. As more and more I learn to love with appreciative love, a few friends or a small community can supply all my needs, while I go out to hundreds or thousands in a love which gives without seeming to receive in return.

Service as Love's Gift

Even if I do not sink into a degenerate need love which uses my friends and my community in a selfish, demanding way, I can fail in another way, which is actually the same thing in disguise. I can take too much for granted the services that others render me, and accept them without any appreciation. In community life, a multitude of hidden and not-so-hidden services are rendered, and I can tend to forget to give recognition to those who serve. I act as though I have such a right to these services that the others have only a duty to render them. I become demanding, complaining, if I think that I detect some deficiency in the service.

This is not the Christian attitude toward services. If I demand service, and harp upon the other's duty to render it, in reality I am only using the other person. It is always unloving and unchristian to use another, or to take advantage of his generosity, even if he is loving and willing in his service.

In Christian community, service is never demanded, and rights to service are not insisted upon. Service is Christian only when it is a gift in love. It is never mere duty, it is always and only love's gift to the body of Christ. Even the most humble service, such as washing dishes or cleaning floors, is a charism building up the body of Christ, when it is inspired by the Holy Spirit and is rendered in love.

But such loving giving is possible only in a context of

loving appreciation of one another as truly brothers and sisters in the Lord. The appreciation in question, we said, is not simply a recognition and acknowledgment of the services, but rather is a love and appreciation of the person serving.

Service should never be required of others except in an atmosphere of appreciation, even when the service is rendered by an employee who receives a just salary for these services. Otherwise the servant is being used as a slave, not appreciated as a brother or sister in Christ. This brother or sister may be crying out in his heart for love. Let us hear that cry. He needs love more than he needs a salary, and in love and justice we give him both love and salary.

If, to be Christian, service is always and only a gift in love, then love's response to this service is more than thanksgiving for what has been done. It is appreciation of the love which serves, and of the person who serves, because of what he is in himself, son of God, brother of Christ.

It is right and just, of course, to accord grateful recognition of the service itself and to express words of thanks. But such recognition is empty if it is not at the same time an expression of the appreciation which is love of the person. There is a subtle difference between lovingly appreciating a person for what he is in himself, and merely recognizing and thanking him for what he does. My superficial "thank you" can really be only a form of using another, giving recognition to his works so that he will do all the more for me. But what he needs above all is love for him as a person, and any "thank you" for his work should be an expression of deep esteem for his person. Any expression of this esteem is a kind of loving praise of what he *is*.

Praise and Thanksgiving

So too in our relationship with God, there is a difference between praise and thanksgiving. Thanksgiving is appreciation of what God *does* for us, praise is joyous appreciation of the marvelous Persons that he *is*. My love *thanks* him for what he does in the world and in my life, my love *praises* him for what he is in himself.

As I praise him, I also thank him for what he is in himself, for what he is in himself is what he wants to be for me! What God wants to be for me is infinitely more valuable than what he gives to me. He wants to be my Father, my Friend, my Bridegroom. To be friend, or bridegroom, or father is to share one's very person with the loved one. Therefore I must take care to go beyond the kind of prayer which expects only things from God and only looks to him so that he can *do* something for me. I must cultivate the kind of prayer which is openness to his very Person and to what he wants to *be* for me.

Worship of God is loving appreciation of the wonderful riches which are his very being, which he opens up to me. My joy in the Lord is joy that he is what he is. Thus his own joy is poured out into me, the joy which the three divine Persons have in their communion with one another.

Appreciation of what he is in his very being is the prayer of loving contemplation. And, of course, the fullness of this loving appreciation is possible only when he pours the grace of contemplation into me, giving me a taste of what he is in himself. I must let neither what he *does* for me, or what I do for him, distract me from what he wants to *be* for me!

Like the Suffering Servant

Perhaps we think that those who serve us in Christian love should not be granted recognition and appreciation, so that they can be like the Suffering Servant Jesus, who continued to serve in love even when he was despised and rejected.

It may indeed be Christian for a person to continue to serve humbly and lovingly even when he is not appreciated as a person, is not granted recognition for what he does, and is even rejected as Jesus was. But it certainly is unchristian not to grant him recognition and not to love and appreciate him.

In serving us in love, even Jesus was looking for a return in love, so that we could find joy in loving him and his Father: "As the Father has loved me, so have I loved you; abide in my love" (Jn 15:9). Abide in my love by accepting it and thus returning it. Give me the joy of letting me love you. Return my love by accepting it, that your joy may be full.

Though he looked for a return of love, Jesus continued to love and serve even when acceptance and appreciation were not accorded him, because he was looking for our eventual response to his love, so that he could fill us with joy in loving communion with him.

Thus, even though a Christian serves with love which does not seek recognition for its own sake, it is Christian to grant him both recognition and appreciation. The full joy of community results only when persons are lovingly appreciated as persons, and persons are thus united in loving communion.

Our Redeeming Love

Appreciative love, rather than sheer need love, is a sign of maturity in love, and should characterize all the mature people in community. Those who serve in mature love render their services as the expression of appreciative love of the persons they serve, looking upon them as brothers and sisters in the Lord.

The lowliest of services, such as scrubbing floors, thus take on the wonderful value of the love in which they are rendered. Whatever I do springs from the beautiful, loving person that I am. The loving person I am renders great dignity and value even to the most humble and insignificant service I render. Love so shines forth from me in everything I do that a response of love springs forth from those I serve, so that all of us are united in love and joy.

My loving service sometimes does meet sinful unlovingness and rejection, just as Jesus, the Suffering Servant, was rejected. But my appreciating love of others never says, "He does not deserve love, there is nothing in him to appreciate." I still love him with the love of appreciation, because he is "the brother for whom Jesus died" (1 Cor 8:11). God loves him and has redeemed him in the blood of his Son.

God does not love us because we are good, we are good because he loves us. He loves us first, and makes us good by loving us. Love is always creative of good. It is not first of all the good qualities of others that make us love them in Christ, but we love them in order to implant and nourish these qualities in them, and thus save them in Christ.

Just as a father's loving appreciation of his child encourages the growth of the child and thus increases his lovableness, so our love even for a sinner has the same effect. Our love brings God's redeeming love to him and makes him worthy of appreciation, for our love invites the response of love which makes him lovable.

Chapter 15

Appreciation Is Akin to Contemplation

To appreciate a person, I have to notice him lovingly, be attentive to him, listen to him. For only in loving attention can I become aware of the marvelous mystery of his being and learn to rejoice in it. Appreciation is thus a kind of contemplation. When I deeply appreciate a person, penetrating to the beauty of his being, I am rejoicing in a wonderful work of the Lord, and I worship God for the beauty he has put into his creature. Appreciative contemplation of a human person is akin to the direct contemplation of God.

The most glorious moments of our life are our moments of appreciation, those moments when we are caught up in the rapturous contemplation of beauty. We turn a bend in the road and suddenly see before us a glorious valley bathed in evening sunlight, and we gasp in rapture at the beauty. We listen to a magnificent symphony, or we gaze upon a beautiful painting, and are filled with a glorious joy. Experiences like this are all the richer when someone we love is with us to share in our appreciation.

Or more wonderful than all this, I look into someone's eyes with love, and am enraptured by the beauty I see in him, and he returns my look with the same rapture over what he sees in me. We are filled with joy as we contemplate and appreciate the beauty of each other as persons.

Moments like these, moments of contemplation and appreciation, are the richest experiences of life. Loving appreciation is the fullness of life. Appreciating human persons and contemplating God are closely related. Both experiences belong to the fullness of life. We do not really know how to live if we do not know how to appreciate and enjoy persons, and if we do not know how to spend time in the prayer which is the appreciation of God.

Both enjoyment of persons and prayerful contemplation of God are necessary for the fullness of community life. Community requires time together to appreciate one another, and time together for appreciating God: time for fellowshipping, and time for community prayer.

Time Together

Community grows when we spend time together enjoying one another. Appreciation requires that we know how to play together, how to have a good time together. Enjoying one another's presence is the expression of our mutual appreciation, and deepens it.

Because it is a time for community love, time together has to have a focus: It is a time for showing appreciation. Love keeps its eyes open to whatever and whoever needs to be appreciated. Only where we are appreciated can we grow in self-confidence in using our gifts well for the good of our fellowmen. Appreciation of persons cannot grow if we never take time to see one another's gifts and talents at work. Therefore we should build into our community life opportunities for contributing to the play and life of the community.

In religious communities, time together has usually been given the name "recreation." Perhaps this is not such a good word for it, since recreation has been explained as re-creation of our powers for work or for prayer. Thus, there has been a tendency to think of recreation only as a means to something else, only as a means to renewal for work. But this is to miss the point that playing together and enjoying one another is a wonderful value in itself. The joy of being with people and appreciating them as persons belongs to the fullness of life, and is no mere means to something else.

Perhaps "fellowshipping" would be a better word to describe this time together for enjoying one another. For our joy in being together as a community is part of the joy of *koinonia,* fellowship, the scriptural term for the communion in life which is of the essence of Christian living (Acts 2:42, 46). In its fuller meaning, of course, fellowshipping is not just having a good time together. It is the sharing of everything in our life, putting all that we are and have at the service of one another. We have to celebrate the joy of this sharing in love. Therefore our life should be seasoned with frequent times together whose whole focus is loving appreciation of one another.

We should not be trying to fit only rare moments of appreciation into very busy lives of work and service, as if we could not afford time for play. We should realize that appreciation is the fullness of life itself, and we should have the joy of being together at some period each day. If we do not take time to appreciate one another, we do not take time to live! If we do not fellowship with one another, then we do not have community. Time together for joy in one another should be a high point of the day.

The same things are true of those other high points of the day, the times of community prayer, in which we gather together to appreciate the Lord God and find joy in his presence. "The joy of the Lord is our strength" (Neh 8:10).

The Relationship of Work and Play

If we are always busy working and never take time to be together, we will miss the point of what work is all about.

There is a certain joy in our work, especially when we use our intelligence and our skills in our work. There is a joy in expressing ourselves by doing things and making things, and a joy of accomplishment. But this is not yet the fullness of joy. The fullness comes when others appreciate and enjoy the fruits of our work, especially when we enjoy these fruits with them, and above all when we ourselves are appreciated as the persons who have produced these fruits. Such appreciation should be the full fruit of all human work.

Thus, at a meal together at the end of the day we celebrate the love which prepared the meal, as well as the love which others have expressed in other ways by serving in their day's work. Or better, the time together and the meal together celebrate the *persons* gathered together in love, who are radiant with the joy of mutual appreciation.

Virtuous Circle

When we regularly take out time for fellowshipping, we soon find that we are caught up into a beautiful virtuous circle. The more we appreciate others through being with them, the more we want to be with them. At first we may have to make an effort to be together. But as we grow in appreciation, more and more we are filled with love's desire for presence with one another.

We should beware of seeing our responsibilities to the community in minimal terms: I have this duty to perform, this service to render. Basic duties and services are only a skeleton upon which a fullness of life must be built. Every member of the community has a responsibility to contribute to this fullness of life by initiating various exchanges and activities which build up the life of the whole body.

I must initiate processes of reconciliation, for example, when there is separation among persons. I must initiate communication when no one seems to be in touch with anyone else. I must initiate get-togethers, such as liturgies for special occasions, or parties to celebrate birthdays and anniversaries, or unusual accomplishments which deserve appreciation.

Each one contributes to the fullness of life in accord with his own special gift. One person is good at liturgical celebrations, another is talented in arranging parties, others can sing or play musical instruments, others can entertain in other ways. Life together is full only when we have this joy of mutual appreciation.

In our time together, I can do many things which will foster mutual appreciation. But above all I have to love, and in love I have to notice others and be interested in them, and listen to them.

Listening to you, I inquire about your day, your joys and problems, your work and your interests. If I am not interested in the good you were able to do today, or in the problems with which you have struggled, then I do not really love you, and we have no community with each other. But if I do love you, my joy in you is manifest in my interest in what you do.

Vicious Circle

When no one appreciates what I try to say, when no one really listens to me when I speak about my day or my work, I become convinced that they have no appreciation of me as a person; and so I keep quiet and withdraw to myself, and we have no community.

Community breaks down when no one is interested in what anyone else is doing. I do not appreciate you because you do not appreciate me. You are not interested in me or my work, so I am not interested in you or yours. You feel unappreciated, and so do I. You are unneeded, and so am I. We are in a vicious circle.

But loving listening leads to deeper appreciation, and appreciation gives rise to renewed listening, and the virtuous circle produces desire for one another's presence. And the joy of being together is established.

Celebrating Fellowship

It is clear, then, that fellowshipping is not just a time for rest from work. It is a summit, a high point in life. It is a celebration of the fruits of work and of the services we have rendered one another in love. Above all, it is the celebration of love, and of the persons we love. It is a source of renewal of life and of love, it is refreshment for taking up anew all the other elements of our communion in life.

Through the loving appreciation which we express in our time together, we build up one another and build up the body of Christ. For loving appreciation builds up the sense of worth of each member of the community, and gives each the courage to undertake life's tasks free of any sense of futility. The various services we render one another, no matter how lowly they are in themselves, take on a wonderful new meaning and value, for in an atmosphere of loving appreciation we become loving persons, eagerly serving in love, expressing our appreciation of others through our various services.

Our prayer together also takes on a new value because of our play together. The mutual appreciation which has been nurtured in our joy in one another's presence is expressed and celebrated anew in community prayer. Our prayer together expresses not only our loving appreciation of the Lord, but also our joy in one another. Even prayer is play, in the sense that it is joy in the Lord's presence, and loving appreciation of who he is.

Appreciation of persons is joy in the greatest works of the Lord, the wonders which he is accomplishing in his people, his children. And he is accomplishing much of this through our loving appreciation, which encourages the growth of those whom we appreciate. Moreover, when I appreciate what the Lord is doing in you, the image of God, I am drawn to the Lord himself. I am drawn to desire heavenly realities, for I contemplate God in one of his most marvelous works, one of his beloved children, image of the heavenly Father.

Out of the fullness of the community's joy in one another springs the community's apostolate to the poor and needy. The goal of all service of the poor, we have seen, is to bring them, too, into the joy of community and friendship.

Chapter 16

Appreciating God in Community Prayer

Just as we need time together to appreciate one another, so we need time together to appreciate the Lord our God. Worship is appreciating the Lord together. Worship is the fullness of community, because appreciating God is the fullness of life.

We can say that the inner life of God himself, the life of the three divine Persons, is mutual appreciation. The fullness of their life is their overflowing joy in one another, their rapturous savoring of one another's divine beauty. Rapturous appreciation of the beauty of a human person is always a high point in our life. The three divine Persons are eternally at the high point of their rapturous joy in one another.

As children of God, we are called to share in this joy which the divine Persons have in one another. To enter heaven is to "enter into the Lord's joy" (Mt 25:21). Even now our worship of God is appreciating in some degree the wonders of the divine Persons which they themselves enjoy to the full. "Rejoice in the Lord always, again I say, rejoice!" (Phil 4:4).

Our appreciation of God can only be in response to his appreciation of us, his manifestation of himself to us in prayer and in community. God appreciates us as his beloved sons and daughters in Jesus his Beloved. We are the brothers and sisters for whom Jesus died, and the Father rejoices in us as his children, lovingly acknowledging us as such in his Son. He addresses his word of love to us, especially in community worship, pouring out his Holy Spirit of love into our hearts, and giving the very Person of his Son to us in the Eucharist.

To appreciate the Lord, I have to be attentive to his presence which he manifests in worship, I have to listen lovingly to his words of love, I have to be receptive to his Holy Spirit. I have to savor the sweetness of his presence in Eucharistic communion, and lovingly rejoice in him.

I can do all this best in communion with others, for I learn to pray by praying with those who pray. I am caught up into the joy of those who are already rejoicing in the Lord. As we appreciate God together, we lead one another ever more deeply into this contemplation.

The Lord's Presence in Community Worship

The full meaning of the Lord's resurrection is his continuing presence in our midst as giver of life. "It is I myself!" Jesus insists as he appears to his disciples on the evening of his resurrection (Lk 24:39). It was impossible for him to be held by death (Acts 2:24). "I am with you always until the end of the world" (Mt 28:20). "Where two or three are gathered in my name, there am I in the midst of them" (Mt 18:20). I am with you as "life-giving Spirit" (1 Cor 15:45), the one who gives you God's own life.

The risen Lord's presence is a spiritual presence, an unseen power-filled reality. It is a presence to us through the Holy Spirit.

But if the Lord is unseen, how is he image (visible

presence) of the invisible God? His unseen spiritual presence is made visible in his body, the Church, which carries on his own mission as image of the invisible God (cf. Eph 3:10).

The Lord's real but unseen presence as he works in us through his Holy Spirit is manifest in the Church in three fundamental ways: in the proclamation and explanation of God's word, in the sacrament of the breaking of the bread, and in the fraternal love uniting his disciples as brothers and sisters. These three manifestations of the Lord's presence are dramatized for us in the story of the disciples of Emmaus (Lk 24:13-33).

In this story we see, first, that the Lord in person was working invisibly in the hearts of the disciples through his Spirit as he opened their minds to understand his word: "Were not our hearts burning within us as he talked to us on the road and explained the scriptures to us?" (Lk 24:32). The Lord in person continues to be present and working and manifest in the Church's ministry of the word.

Secondly, the Lord himself, working invisibly in their hearts through his Spirit, was the source of the fraternal love in which the two disciples urged their hospitality upon the One whom they thought was a stranger (Lk 24:29). "Those with whom Truth walked could not be far from love," says St. Gregory (PL 76:1182). The fraternal love of Christians is a visible sign of Christ's personal presence in their midst as the source of this love.

Thirdly, they recognized the invisible presence of the Lord "in the breaking of the bread" (Lk 24:31, 35). The Lord, ever present in our midst, is manifest and operative in a most striking way in the Eucharist.

Though the Lord disappeared from their bodily sight as soon as they recognized him in the breaking of the bread, the disciples were not at all saddened by this disappearance. Rather, they rejoiced greatly, for the whole incident had made them vividly aware of the continuing spiritual presence of the risen Lord.

All three manifestations of the invisible Lord are integral elements of every Eucharistic celebration: word, sacrament, and fraternal love. These three manifestations are given only in the Christian community, the people which continues the Lord's mission as image of the invisible God. In responding to the Lord present and manifest in the community, we are responding to the invisible God himself.

Stemming from these basic manifestations are many other manifestations of God in the Christian community. We have already spoken of several of these in showing how each member of the Church carries on in his own way the Lord's mission as image of God; fathers are image of God to their children, husbands and wives are image of God for one another.

The praying community is an image of God in a very full way, and all the elements in the community's prayer coalesce to complete the image in which God manifests his presence and in which we respond to him. The following reflections upon what takes place in Christian community worship make it clear that in the assembly we respond directly to the Lord in person who is really present. What we shall say is true not only of the Church's official liturgy, such as the Eucharistic celebration, but also of prayer meetings such as those conducted in charismatic communities. These meetings supplement the Eucharistic liturgy, and do not replace it.

Response to the Lord in Community Praise

First, community praise, acclamation of the Lord, is a direct recognition of the Lord who is there. He promised to be in the midst wherever two or three are gathered together in his name (Mt 18:20). Those gathered together in living faith take him at his word, they claim what he promised, they touch his presence!

Indeed, the basic act of Christian faith is recognition of the Lord and surrender to him, saying like Thomas, "My Lord and my God!" (Jn 20:28). This recognition and acceptance of the Lord are an acclamation, a joyous greeting of him who is present with us: "My Lord and my God!" He is always in our midst. You do not have to go up to the heavens to bring Christ down, says St. Paul (Rm 10:6), or go down into the abyss to bring Christ up. No, he is with you. He is as close to you as the word of faith which you believe and profess. "For if you confess with your lips that Jesus is Lord, and believe in your heart that God raised him from the dead, you will be saved" (Rm 10:9).

But Thomas' recognition of the risen Lord is granted to him only in the midst of the community. Because the other brothers in the Lord have said to him, "We have seen the Lord!" (Jn 20:25), Thomas is again with them. Their witness amounts to saying, "Come and see!" (Jn 1:46; 4:29). Proclamation of the Lord by those who have seen him leads to acclamation of the Lord by new believers as well as by old ones.

Thus, the fundamental prayer of the Christian community is praise and acclamation of the Lord who is present, just as this is the fundamental act of faith.

That is why for over 15 centuries the Church has always begun its official morning liturgy with the Invitatory, an invitation to acclaim the Lord who is there in the midst.

In this little liturgical ceremony, one person sings the Ninety-fifth Psalm, inviting the whole community to praise: "Come, let us sing joyfully to the Lord! Let us acclaim the rock of our salvation. Let us greet him with thanksgiving. Let us joyfully sing psalms to him" (Ps 95:1-2). After each verse of the psalm, the whole community responds with an acclamation of the Lord, present in our midst in the person of the risen Jesus, head of the community. Throughout the

Easter season, for example, the acclamation refrain used with the psalm is, "The Lord is truly risen, alleluia!"

We know that he is risen, because he is really with us. We experience his presence in the Liturgy of the Word, in the breaking of the bread, in our brotherly love for one another, and in many other ways.

Charismatic communities springing up all over the world are rediscovering that the basic Christian prayer is this praise and acclamation of the Lord who is present in our midst.

Sign of the Spirit's Presence

This direct recognition and acclamation of the Lord is possible, however, only because of the direct personal witness of the Holy Spirit in the heart of each one who sincerely acclaims the Lord. "No one can say 'Jesus is Lord' except in the Holy Spirit" (1 Cor 12:3). Like Jesus, we thrill with joy in the Holy Spirit (Lk 10:21) as we thank the Father for revealing the mystery of his Son, and thereby revealing himself as Father.

St. John too tells us that the first sign that we possess the Holy Spirit and are in communion with God is our acceptance of Jesus, the Son of God: "This is how you can recognize God's Spirit: every spirit that acknowledges Jesus Christ come in the flesh belongs to God" (1 Jn 4:2). The acclamation of the Lord Jesus in the surrender of joyous faith and praise is a striking sign of the presence of the invisible Spirit of God in the hearts of the believers. We experience the presence of the Holy Spirit in this sign which he produces in us, our wholehearted surrender to Jesus in loving faith. "For no one can say 'Jesus is Lord' except in the Holy Spirit" (1 Cor 12:3).

Jesus had said the same thing at the Last Supper when he declared: "The Spirit of truth will bear witness to me, and you also will bear witness to me" (Jn 15:26ff.). Your witness is not possible without his interior witness in your hearts. "He will glorify me, for he will take what is mine and declare it to you. All that the Father has is mine" (Jn 16:14ff.). The Spirit shows us the Father in showing us Jesus. Thus in Jesus and his Spirit we have direct access to the Father (Eph 2:18), the God who is not far off, but who fills all in all (Eph 4:6).

Therefore, through the centuries the Church has begun its Eucharistic liturgy, at least on the Lord's Day, with the acclamation of the Holy Trinity, singing, "Glory to God in the highest." When Christians arouse one another to acclaim the Lord God in praise, Father, Son and Holy Spirit, there is a new release of the power of the Holy Spirit who already dwells in their hearts.

Any time two or three gather together in the name of Jesus for prayer, they should begin by inviting one another to praise and acclaim the Lord who is in their midst. Private prayer, too, should begin with praise: "Our Father . . . hallowed be thy name!"

Response to the Lord Present in His Word

In Spirit-filled praise, then, the worshiping community responds directly to the Lord himself present in their midst. They remain with him in a loving and listening relationship, listening to his love. For when they have surrendered to his presence in faith and praise, they are open to hear his word. Listening to the word is direct attention to the Lord who is present, and is appreciation of his Person.

Prayer is appreciation of the Lord who speaks to us. We listen to him with our whole being and savor what we hear. In savoring the word, pondering it in our hearts, we taste the sweetness of the Lord himself, present to us in his word. In appreciating what we hear, we are eager for more, and thus we invite from him more to listen to. Home is where everyone listens. We are at home with God when we listen to his love speaking to us. When we respond in love, we call forth from his heart his further communication with us, his deepening love for us, his growing appreciation of the beautiful persons we are becoming through our appreciative response to him.

He is ever listening for our response as we listen to his word, and thus we are involved with him in a beautiful circle of love. He listens to us appreciatively, and in his deepening love for us, calls anew to us more deeply, more lovingly, than before; and we respond with a still deeper love and joy in him. The mutual appreciation grows ever deeper, and our life becomes ever fuller.

The Lord speaks to his people in the community assembly through the ministry of the word. The ministry of the word takes other authentic forms in addition to the ministry of the word as exercised in the official liturgy of the Church. The charismatic word-graces manifest in a charismatic prayer meeting, for example, also constitute an authentic ministry or service in building up the body, the Church. These graces are among those which Vatican II officially recognized, urging pastors to acknowledge and encourage them (*Constitution in the Church* 12).

For in these charisms the Holy Spirit is at work. "Now there are varieties of gifts, but the same Spirit, and there are varieties of service, but the same Lord, and there are varieties of workings, but it is the same God who inspires them in everyone" (1 Cor 12:6). God himself is present, speaking in the scriptural readings and in the prophetic and teaching charisms which are so operative in charismatic communities.

Love's Requirements

In the ministry of the word, the Lord personally explains the requirements of love to his people who have surrendered themselves to him in loving praise. Surrendered to him, they must remain in his love. "If you keep my commandments, you will abide in my love, just as I have kept my Father's commandments and abide in his love" (Jn 15:10). And all his commandments are summed up in one. "This is my commandment, that you love one another as I have loved you" (Jn 15:12).

Only if we have been faithful to his word in our daily life, loving one another as he has loved us, do we verify the sincerity and truth of the words of praise in which we acclaim the Lord in faith. "For not everyone who says to me 'Lord, Lord' shall enter the kingdom of heaven, but he who does the will of my Father who is in heaven" (Mt 7:21).

It is the Father's will that we love not only our friends, but even our enemies, "so that you may be sons of your Father in heaven, who makes his sun rise on the evil and on the good, and sends rain on the just and on the unjust" (Mt 5:45).

Ask Whatever You Will

Likewise his word expresses the requirements to be fulfilled if we are to claim his promises in the prayer of faith. "If you remain in me, and my words remain in you, ask whatever you will, and it will be done for you" (Jn 15:7). In telling us to ask whatever we will, Jesus has no fear that we will ask the wrong things, because he knows that his word dwelling in us will form our hearts to ask and desire only the things he has really promised. The only promises we can claim in the prayer of faith are expressed in his word which manifests his loving will. Hence, we pray only within his will. "This is the confidence we have in him, that if we ask anything according to his will, he hears us" (1 Jn 4:14).

That is why the Church for centuries has introduced the Lord's Prayer in the Eucharistic liturgy by saying, *"Formed*

by God's word, we dare to say, 'Our Father . . .' " To claim
God's promises in the prayer of faith, we must be formed
by God's word in the Lord's own image as Son, praying
not only in his words, but in his own living prayer, his personal relationship with the Father in the Holy Spirit. Enlightened by his words and enflamed by his love, we desire
in Jesus only the glory of the Father: "Hallowed be thy
name!" The Father is glorified in his Son to the extent that
all his sons and daughters are "conformed to the image of
his Son" (Rm 8:29).

Formed by his word dwelling in us, our worldly desires
and petitions will fade away. Ever more heavenly desires
will be inspired by the Spirit, and expressed in Christ's
name.

Formed by his word, we live in brotherly love. From
the midst of this love we ask with that prayer of faith which
boldly and unhesitatingly claims his promise. "If two of
you agree on earth about anything they ask, it will be done
for them by my Father in heaven" (Mt 18:19). Charismatic communities have been experiencing in a remarkable
way this power of united prayer.

Appreciating One Another in Community Prayer

God saves us as a community, a people in loving communion with him and with one another. Therefore in
community prayer we appreciate together not only the three
divine Persons, but also the human persons with whom we
share in the joy of the divine Persons.

As image of God on earth, our community life is appreciation of one another, just as the inner life of God is the
mutual appreciation of the three divine Persons. The chief
value we appreciate in one another is each one's beauty as
son or daughter of God, child of God lovingly appreciated
by the heavenly Father, called by him to the direct appreciation of him as Father, and of Jesus as Brother, and of the

Holy Spirit as intimate Spouse of the heart.

In community prayer, we are united in the mutual appreciation in which God appreciates his children and they appreciate him and one another. The deeper our appreciation of God himself, the deeper is our appreciation of one another as called to the same experience. In the presence of God we learn to reverence one another.

An important element in our community prayer, then, is our appreciation of what God is doing in those with whom we pray. Appreciation of the God-given beauty of our brothers and sisters in the Lord, we said, is akin to direct contemplation of God himself. We so appreciate one another as children of God that we honor and praise God for the beauty he is forming in them. In community worship, therefore, we rejoice not only in the Lord himself, but we rejoice in all whom we love and appreciate in the Lord.

This is one of the reasons for witnessing publicly in the midst of the worshiping community to what God has done for us. The charismatic prayer communities are in close harmony with the scriptures when they do this. "Hear now, all you who fear God, while I declare what he has done for me. . . . Blessed be God who refused me not my prayer or his kindness!" (Ps 66:16,20). "O God, in the vast assembly I made no secret of your kindness and your truth. . . . Many shall look on in awe, and trust in the Lord" (Ps 40:11,4). When one publicly praises God in humility for the favors he has received, others are inspired to trust in God and praise him.

Thus, fitting praise of God includes adequate appreciation of his present-day saints among whom we live, the ones he is forming here and now in our midst. "God is wonderful in his holy ones" (Ps 68:36v). This is simply another way of appreciating persons as persons: "Rejoice with those who rejoice!" (Rm 12:15). This is a fitting part of community prayer, for we rejoice in the holiness which God is forming in our brothers and sisters by bringing them with us into his own life and joy. When we appreciate one another in this Christian way, we better appreciate the Lord. "He who is mighty has done great things for me, and holy is his name!" (Lk 1:49). To rejoice with God's holy ones whether they are on earth or in heaven is part of Christian love.

The Lord's community, then, is a virtuous circle. Filled with the Lord's own Holy Spirit, his people are image and presence of God, revealing him to one another. They respond to the Lord manifest to them in the word they proclaim to one another, in the Bread they break and share, in the brotherly love in which they are united. Their love for one another as brothers and sisters in the Lord is the fullness of their filial response to God the Father, imaged to them in the Lord and his people. Their love for one another, in turn, reveals him anew, drawing others into the circle, where these too acclaim the Lord who is there.

Part 5

Community Reconciliation

Chapter 17

Sin Destroys Community

"They heard the sound of the Lord God walking in his garden in the cool of the day" (Gn 3:8). God was coming to enjoy loving communion with the man and woman whom he had created and had brought into his garden to live in his presence (Gn 2:15).

In his story about Adam and Eve, the author of Genesis is telling me what I already know deep in my heart—that I was created for love and joy. I cannot live without love. I was made for communion with God and for the joy which springs from it. I was meant to live in God's presence, completely at home with him, unashamed and without fear. "The man and his wife were both naked, and were not ashamed" (Gn 2:25). Unafraid of God, completely trusting in him and in one another, they felt fully at home, living in openness to God, to each other, and to the world about them.

Such was the significance of their unashamed nakedness. They had nothing to hide, they needed no defenses against each other, they had no fear of self-revelation, for they could trust fully in one another's loving acceptance.

That is how God meant me to be, completely at home with him and with all my fellowmen.

How then did I end up in fear of God, ashamed to be in his presence, hiding from him, not at all at home with him, and uncomfortable and fearful with my fellowmen?

Sin did this to me.

When I sin, I destroy love and community. I bring about division and opposition. I end up alone and lonely, without joy. No man can live without love and joy. Without joy I have no taste for life. Without joy, my energy and strength drain away like water. Sin, separation, loneliness, joylessness inevitably lead to death.

But why do I sin, if sin is so devastating, so death-dealing, so fatal to love and happiness?

Experiencing Sin in Its Fruits

In sinning, I do not fully know what I am doing. For in my act of sin, I deceive myself into thinking that I am doing right and good. I am very clever at this self-deception, at finding reasons to justify what I want. Like David, after his sin with Bathsheba and his murder of her husband, Uriah, I am blind to my sin and to the evil that it does to others. When the prophet Nathan depicts my sin to me in the parable about the rich man who stole the poor man's lamb, like David I become furious with the rich man, the sinner—until the prophet points directly at me and says, "You are that man!" (2 Sm 12:7).

Because of my blindness about my sin and my sinfulness, I begin to experience the full reality of sin only when others in turn sin against me. Only when I am on the receiving end of sin do I begin to understand what sin really is. I am like David when his son Absalom turned his sword against him, just as David had used the sword against Uriah.

When I suffer from the sins of others, perhaps at last I

will open my eyes to understand what I have done to my neighbor by my own sins. Like David, will I forgive my son Absalom as God has forgiven me? Or will I turn against my Absalom in revenge, and thus deepen the divisions already existing among men? Will I reinforce the vicious circle of sin in which we are all trapped?

I experience sin in the pain and divisions and misery it causes. I experience sin in my fear of being unloved, unwanted, unappreciated. I experience sin in the hurting and loneliness within me, in the joylessness which is the fruit of sin, in the unanswered cry of my heart for love. I experience sin in my fear of others, my fear of being hurt if I open myself to them. So I hide, clothing my vulnerability not in fig leaves, but in a hard shell of fear and self-pity.

I am pained by my nakedness, my vulnerability. I am forever running away from the pain of difficult relationships. Consequently, soon I have no relationships at all, no love and communion with others. I am alone. Sin destroys community, and lack of community leads to further sin.

The Vicious Circle of Sin

Sin is usually response to sin. Others have sinned against me, and ever so many of my own sins are a reaction against these sins committed against me. Thus indeed I am caught in a vicious circle.

All sin against me is a failure to love me, a failure to appreciate and reverence me in my true dignity as a human person and child of God. Because others do not love and appreciate me, I in turn fail to love them. I too become a sinner. I resent those who have not loved me, and I choose to sin in return. I set up defenses to protect myself from the pain I receive. Thus I cut myself off from the very possibility of the love I need and desire. I am trapped in the deathly circle. How badly our world needs love and community as the preventive of sin!

Wherever there is no community in love, sin must certainly be there. But where love and community prevail, God is certainly there. If we have no community life, or if our community life is sickly, sin must be present. We must discover these sins, unmask them, expel them.

Fear as Cause of Sin

My basic reaction to lack of love and appreciation is the fear of being unloved and unlovable, the fear of being worthless. This fear in turn is the root of many of my sins. I react against others not only when I fear they will injure me, but even when I fear they will not love me. Many a person would rather be injured than ignored!

Most of my sins against love and community result not from hatred, but from fear of being unloved. Hatred is an ultimate sin against love, whereas fear is a very common beginning of such sins.

The fear of being unloved leads me to sin in many ways. In fear of my worthlessness, I fear I will be rejected if I approach others, and therefore I draw into my shell and make no effort to love them. In fear of being hurt, I stay to myself, I fail to go out to others. Thus I sin against my responsibility to love, and I fail to work toward community. Consequently divisions deepen, because others, in turn, react to me in an adverse way.

Cut off from the love of others, I fall into various sins by which I try to compensate myself for the lack of love which I am experiencing.

Unloved, perhaps I fall into the sin of greed, trying to console myself for lack of love by amassing for myself all kinds of possessions and fine things.

Or perhaps I try to compensate myself for lack of love by falling into sins of lust. I console myself by indulging in sinful solitary sexual pleasure. Or I use another person solely for my own pleasure.

Or I compensate myself for lack of love by gluttony, indulging in excessive eating and drinking, trying to comfort my body in this way, since my whole person is starved for love and affection.

One form of gluttony is addiction to medicines, trying to find comfort in aspirin or Alka Seltzer, or in stronger drugs, or in the use of alcohol. Much of our drug and alcohol problem is due ultimately to the lack of love and appreciation in family life and in contemporary society.

Another compensation for lack of love is anger. I try to manifest my worth by asserting myself in aggressiveness, returning injury for injury. Or if I am weak and fearful, I react in defensiveness. This may be only another form of aggressiveness, for though I seem to be withdrawn into a protective shell, nevertheless I keep striking out against others in a number of ways. I attack them by subtle innuendo, instead of bringing my hurts and grievances directly into the open. Were I to talk out my problems with the others, I could be healed more quickly. How often I am defensive against an injury which the other party does not even know he has inflicted, and which he did not intend to inflict. Open communication with others saves me from many unnecessary hurts.

Or again, to compensate for my feelings of worthlessness, my fear of being an unloved nobody, I put on a false front of bravado, displaying my talents, boasting of my accomplishments. Or I become belligerent, asserting either my muscle or my intellectual superiority to show that I am really better than others. Consequently I come through as proud, independent, self-sufficient, self-righteous in asserting my worth. Therefore others resist me all the more, and I defeat my very purpose of being someone worthwhile and lovable.

Deep down, my whole being is crying out for love and

appreciation. But all that others see are my offensive ways of acting. They react to my actions, instead of responding lovingly to my inner cry for love and healing.

All of us who claim to be Christian need to learn how to detect and listen to the deeper cry for love and affection which is so often expressing itself in the sins of those around us. How many sins are rooted in the fear of being unloved and worthless! We should learn to respond to this fear, this cry for love, rather than to the actions in which a person tries to compensate for his starved affections. Instead of responding to his aggressiveness with aggressiveness, or to his defensiveness with defensiveness, I should respond to his deep-seated neediness with compassion, support and real love.

Are not our fellowmen so greedy for material riches and comforts, and do they not indulge in gluttony and drinking, in drugs and in sex, in violence and destruction, in boasting and belligerence, chiefly because we have neglected to give them the love and fellowship and forgiveness which they need so badly? Have we not forced them to waste on the wrong things their wonderful God-given power to love, because by our lack of love and concern for them we have not drawn forth love from their hearts? Loving community is the remedy for the multitude of sins tearing our society apart.

The Fear Behind Pride

If no one has given me love and friendship, to compensate myself I may try to take possession of someone, trying to force his love. But love can never be extorted. It can only be given willingly. And so my efforts to possess another are not love, but tyranny. I do not love him, I use him. I manipulate him for my own purposes. Instead of winning his love, I drive him away.

Since I cannot extort love, I may try to console myself

by exerting power and control over others. How much of my proud ambition to domineer over others, and my lust for prestige and success, is simply a compensation for my failure to win love and to enjoy community.

My very ambition to get ahead has a way of killing whatever love I may have had. In my fear of being a nobody, I compensate myself by trying to win a name for myself, or by trying to win power in the world. I justify all this by telling myself that I am doing this to win good things for those I love, my wife and family. But in reality I am so busy trying to get ahead that I have no time for my family and my community. So love dies out of my life. I compensate for this by an ever-increasing grasp for power or acclaim. The vicious circle of unlove and sin deepens.

"The Pride of the We"

In pride I try to compensate for my fear of being unloved in either of two ways, depending upon whether I am strong or weak. If I am unloved but strong, I exert power over others, using them, controlling and manipulating them. But if I am weak and conscious of my nothingness, I am likely to fall into "the pride of the we," the collective pride of the group with which I have associated myself: my country club circle, my little clique or false community, whose only bond of unity, perhaps, is our common search for security in what we do as a group, or in our sense of belonging. I fear to come out of this closed circle of my own kind, and so I am not open to the joy of the broader Christian community.

Ever so many divisions in community result from our failure to appreciate others and let them be themselves. We resent others because they are different than we are. We should rather rejoice when others are other than we are. For their ideas and talents and viewpoints and ways of doing things bring an added richness to our community which we of ourselves cannot bring. If I and my friends enrich the community in one way, they and their friends enrich it in another way. In this we all rejoice, because we are all one body under one Head; and all that is mine is yours, and what is yours is mine.

The collective pride of the weak is more enduring and more disastrous than the individualistic pride of the strong, for collective pride hides easily behind a mask of individual humility and unselfish service to a good cause. The unity in pride masquerades as unity in love. A religious community, for example, may be hiding its present inadequacies by glorying in the past history of the order.

A charismatic community, too, can fall into the pride of the we, leading to division from others not of the group. Thus, the charismatic church at Corinth split up into factions. "This is what I mean: One of you will say, 'I belong to Paul,' another, 'I belong to Apollos,' still another, 'Cephas has my allegiance,' and the fourth, 'I belong to Christ'" (1 Cor 1:12ff.). Even if a community does not split into factions, in its very unity it can be guilty of the pride of the we.

The remedy is to be fully open to all our fellowmen outside our community, recognizing the good in others, rejoicing in the work God is doing in them, as well as what he is doing among us. We have no monopoly on the Holy Spirit. We must realize that of ourselves, whether individually or collectively, we are no better than others, and everything we have is the gift of God's love and mercy.

We must examine ourselves, asking, is our sense of belonging to a wonderful community only a subtle form of pride masking our personal inadequacies and weaknesses, which we refuse to accept in humility and patience, or which we refuse to conquer by carrying on the good fight in Christ. Authentic humility accepts the truth of our own nothingness, and knows how to ask and receive in humble love. In love we know how to accept help as well as how to give it. We are all beggars before God, and we receive his generous gifts through one another.

False community covers up inadequacies in the pride of the we, but true community fully develops each of its members so that there are no inadequacies, in the sense that each is using his gifts, each is making his contribution for the good of all. When each is doing his part in giving, each is lovingly and humbly receiving as well.

In humility we have to know how to wait patiently for growth, not trying to force the fruits of prayer, of service, of virtue, of education. A community of love knows how to be patient with the imperfect. But only in an atmosphere of love and appreciation does growth come surely and steadily.

I Am Not Guiltless

Even though many of my sins are a reaction to the failure of others to love and appreciate me, I am not thereby excused from sin. For my reaction is itself a failure to love. I myself thereby become a sinner like the sinners who have not loved me.

Often my reactions of resentment of those who have not loved me is a worse sin than their failure to love. For sometimes the other's failure to love is due not to malice and enmity, but simply to thoughtlessness, negligence, busyness about many things. I must be careful never to resent what another has done to me, or has failed to do for me. My heart must learn to pay attention, not to what he has done or has failed to do, but to the reasons why he has so acted. Perhaps he too is crying out for love and esteem, and his external actions betray his preoccupation with self-worth and being lovable. Perhaps he has neglected me and has been unable to love and notice me because he too is still enslaved by his fears and his self-pity, and cannot go out of himself to others.

When I see sin in another, I should not conclude that he is vicious. I should rather look deeper, listen more closely, and perhaps I will discover that the sinner is like a frightened child. I must try to understand others' fears. Even hatred and malice are sometimes only the last bitter fruit of being unloved.

Instead of reacting to his offense against me by unlovingness to him, I should respond rather to his deeper need for love and forgiveness. He can live without love no more than I can. So I must love him.

Since all of us by our very thoughtlessness and negligence hurt others so easily, we must take great care to be thoughtful of others, going out of our way to show love to everyone, to converse with them, to listen to them as they tell of their interests. How much good a smile or a touch of affection can do, in reassuring others that they are loved and lovable!

There is never any excuse for my unloving reaction to someone's lack of love for me. For Christ my Redeemer can always heal my hurt, and can give me power to love even those who reject me. To love even my enemies is not impossible; it is divine!

If I fall into self-pity, turning in upon myself, feeling sorry for myself because I have not been loved, I sin anew, and close myself to God's love which is ever ready to embrace me. My self-pity and discouragement are a sin against trust in his love. His love for me is ever steadfast and faithful.

But who will help me to trust in his love? Who will show forth his love to me? This is the task of Christian community, and of everyone in the community. If I am to be healed of my sinful ambitions, of my greed and gluttony, of my selfish using of others, of my lustful efforts to possess them, then I need to experience genuine love in a healthy, forgiving Christian community. I need community love in which Christ's own love is poured out to me by my brothers and sisters in the Lord. I need a community in which I forgive those who have not loved me, and in which God and the community forgive me because I have not loved them.

But if my fellowmen, my friends, my community do not seem to be giving me the love and support I need, the Lord himself will not let me down. He is ever faithful to me. If I am faithful to him, open to him in complete trust, he will be able to open his heart to me. He is my rock, my love, my joy. I must focus my life totally on him.

Fears of Senior Citizens

We have been trying to show how fear and insecurity give rise to so many of our sins against love and community. Many of the sins of senior citizens result from their fear of increasing worthlessness. They see that they are being displaced from positions of service and importance which they held. They see that their physical and mental powers are failing because of their advancing age. They see that the little world they had worked so hard to build is crumbling before the bulldozers of a new generation, which is building another little world of its own.

In their resulting fear of worthlessness and rejection, older people can fall into sins of adamant opposition to change, sins of resentment of the young and envy of their success, sins of anger and irritability, of criticism and interference, sins of sabotage of the plans of the young and discouragement of their hopes, sins of failure to recognize and encourage the charisms of the young.

To help remedy these sins of the elderly, the younger people should recognize the fears of worthlessness and rejection which give rise to them, and should meet these fears with love and appreciation. The elderly should be loved and appreciated for their own sake, for their dignity as children of God, for their dedication and labors and accomplishments of the past. Their fears of worthlessness should be dispelled by a genuine interest in them, and a loving concern for them. This interest and concern should take care to provide them with real opportunities to be of service to others. Ways should be found to let them use their talents.

There is never a part of the body of Christ which is not needed.

Fears of the Young

The young have their own kinds of fears and sins. They fear lack of approval by their elders. Their fear of failure leads them to discouragement and abandonment of projects, or to lack of patience in awaiting fruits. Their discouragement must be allayed by others who love and appreciate them, and what they are trying to do.

Fear of condemnation and lack of approval can lead to resentment and rebellion. The remedy is listening to the ideas of the young, discerning what is truly worthwhile in their projects. The young must be allowed to be their true selves, not forced into preconceived notions of what they should be. They should not be judged by the past, but by the present of which they are the product. We should listen to their hearts, to discern the new hopes which God himself has planted in their hearts to meet the new times. We should be attentive to the charisms which God has given them for building up the body of Christ in a way adapted to a new era of salvation history.

Fear of Criticism

Young and old alike, as well as those in between, are ever plagued by fear of criticism by others. This fear leads to the sin of discouragement and the abandonment of projects and responsibilities which would promote love and community. Criticism and correction can easily be interpreted as rejection and lack of love. Such an interpretation is justified when the correction does not proceed from true fraternal love. Only too often we correct another not from love of him or concern for his true welfare, but simply because his defects annoy or hinder us. When criticism does proceed from love, it must nevertheless be administered in such a way that it is not purely negative. It must be given in the context of encouragement, to minimize the danger of wounded self-confidence.

Fear as the Root of Envy

Another form of fear which leads me to sin against community love is my fear of those who are more gifted than I am. This fear causes me to envy. In fear of my own worthlessness, I fear that others will outshine me and will show up my nothingness in sharp contrast. Envy is sadness over the other's blessings, which I see as a threat to myself.

Envy is a sin against love, because true love always appreciates and rejoices in the welfare and happiness of others. All the blessings of others are my blessings, too, because, says St. Augustine, we are all one body under one head, Jesus Christ.

Envy, or sadness over another's blessings, leads me to sins of calumny, detraction, carping criticism, and the like, by which I try to deprive the other of his excellence. Calumny is the malicious uttering of false charges or misrepresentations to damage another's reputation. Detraction is the denial of another's good qualities. Carping criticism is forever looking only for the other's defects, instead of rejoicing in his goodness. All these are sins against the love and appreciation which I owe to others.

When I am envious, and tearing down people, deep down in my heart I am probably crying out for love and appreciation, even while I am meting out the opposite of this to others.

The best remedy for envy, of course, is a rich community life in which everyone is loved and appreciated, and everyone's feelings of worthlessness are counteracted by his opportunities to let his own gifts and love have full play in the service of others.

Negative Humor

Another form of fear which paralyzes love and community is the fear of being laughed at, the fear of the negative humor which pokes fun at my shortcomings.

There is no place for negative humor in Christian life, even though we often try to justify it by claiming that it is an expression of affection for the other. It may very well be. The shortcomings of someone we love are often part of the charm of his person. But even though we laugh at them in good humor, nonetheless we hurt the loved one by this kind of humor.

Sloth: Fear of Love's Cost

If it is true that so much of our sin is reaction to the failure of others to love us, where did this vicious circle start? Why did someone fail to love in the first place? Because this somebody or these somebodies were unwilling to pay the high cost of loving.

No one wants to be lonely and unloved. No one really wants to be unloving. Yet it costs something to love, and I tend to draw lines limiting how far I will go in sharing with others.

Once again, fear is at the root of this failure to love. I fear the cost of loving. I fear to surrender myself in love, because I am afraid that in loving I will lose something I hold dear. I fear that it will cost me my independence, my comfort, my possessions. This is true both in regard to love of God and love of my brothers in community.

The joy which I would find in love is replaced by sadness over the cost of loving. This sadness causes loss of enthusiasm, and saps away my vitality. Thus I end up in the sin of sloth.

Sloth is sadness over the cost of loving. Sadness causes heaviness and inertia. Sloth is aversion to exertion, it is disinclination to action or to labor, and therefore it leads to unwillingness to love. As sadness over the price of loving, it is a sin against love and joy.

Obviously, sloth is an obstacle to community. It draws definite lines as to how far it will go in loving and giving, and its limits become ever more narrow, for failure to love shrinks the capacity to love. My sloth says, "Don't bother me now!" no matter how badly the other needs my love and attention. I say this not only to my fellowmen. I say it even to God when he invites me to prayer and intimacy with him.

Sloth leads to all sorts of sins of negligence and omission. Of course, the slothful one never has any sins to confess. He says, "I didn't do anything," meaning "I did no wrong actions." I committed no positive acts of injury or violence, robbery or theft, lust or gluttony. I harmed no one.

He thinks he is good because he has done no harm. But he should say, "I did nothing good." I failed to love. I am guilty of omission. We will be condemned by Jesus for our failure to do good. "I was hungry and you did not feed me, naked and you did not clothe me. I invited you to intimacy with me, and you did not spend time with me in prayer."

Sloth leads to an ever-increasing inability to love God and fellowmen. The most deadening sin of all is apathy, the last degree of sloth. Apathy is total insensitivity to others and their needs, and insensitivity to the word and invitation of God. It is insensitivity to love. It is a hopelessness and powerlessness that do nothing at all. They are worse than hatred, in a way, because hatred is at least powerful, and can still be turned to love.

Every type of sin, of course, weakens our power to love. The helplessness in which I am held captive when I am caught in the vicious circle of sin calls for the redeeming power of Christ and his healing love. His love heals me of the wounds I have suffered because I have not been loved, and also of the wounds I have inflicted upon myself by reacting against this lack of love, and by falling into the sin of self-pity.

Christ's love is brought to me in the sacrament of Penance, and in the loving forgiveness granted to me in community by my brothers and sisters. We celebrate this redeeming and healing love in every Eucharistic liturgy. "Fear not, O Zion, be not discouraged! The Lord your God is in your midst, a mighty savior. He will rejoice over you with gladness, and renew you in his love" (Zep 3:16ff.).

The Lord's own joy in receiving sinners back has to be manifested in the loving joy of the community gathered together in the presence of the Lord. "The Lord's joy is my strength" (Neh 8:10). Sadness, sloth, saps away our strength and courage. The joy of God's own love poured out into our hearts brings the fortitude and endurance necessary in paying the price of dying to self in loving others.

Complacency

Perhaps some of my readers have been thinking, "When is he going to stop talking about all these fears, these sins of the immature? Maybe they aren't even sins, but are simply immaturity!"

Even if they were merely immaturity, all these fears would still need the healing and redeeming grace of Christ given to us in the sacrament of Penance, for they all involve a spiritual helplessness which hinders our power to love and serve. Therefore they should be brought to the Redeemer, who is present to us with his healing power in the sacrament of Penance and reconciliation. As long as we are fearful and joyless, it is clear that the Lord's redeeming work in us is far from accomplished, and therefore we need his redeeming presence in the sacrament of Penance.

The grace of healing, however, like every grace, brings a responsibility. In this case, the responsibility is to put the redeeming grace to work in fighting the good fight and winning the victory over the disorder and wounds left in us by sin and by immaturity.

If I think that I am spiritually mature because I seem to commit none of these sins stemming from fear, then perhaps I am guilty of the sin of complacency. Complacency is another form of sloth. It is self-satisfaction with what I have already accomplished. It is a refusal to go higher, it is getting into a rut on the plateau which I have reached, and never scaling the greater heights of love. It is living in one's comfortable way of spirituality, and thus not hearing God's call to greater things. It is holding on so tightly to God's earliest graces that one's hands are not open to receive his greater gifts.

It is a fear of giving up what I have, because I am well satisfied with myself, and so it is unwillingness to let go of the earlier stages in my life in order to grow into new and richer stages.

It is trust in my own perfection and is lack of trust in God, who can fill me with his more precious gifts only when I have emptied myself of his preliminary gifts, which I should now leave behind, to receive more fully than ever before his gift of himself, the uncreated grace.

Chapter 18

The Sacrament of Community Reconciliation

Everyone in the Christian community has the power to forgive sins. Each little boy can forgive his little sister when she has hurt him. Each daughter can forgive her mother if the mother has been negligent. Parents can forgive their children for disobedience, and children can ask for this forgiveness. Each husband can forgive his wife. Each wife can forgive her mother-in-law. Each adolescent and each young adult can forgive the generations which have gone before them and have brought the world to its present sorry state.

It is not enough for God to forgive sinners and bring them back. All God's people must also forgive them and receive them back. We can be at peace with God only in peace with one another. "There is but one body and one Spirit, just as there is but one hope given all of you by your call" (Eph 4:4).

If I do not forgive, I only deepen the separations which divide mankind, I worsen the disorder in the world, I make myself as bad or worse than those who went before me.

Ready willingness to forgive is necessary if I myself am to be forgiven by God. If I must forgive in order to receive

God's forgiveness, then it follows that I can forgive, that I do have power to forgive sins. When I forgive, God's own forgiveness is working and manifest, for God's own Holy Spirit in our hearts moves us to forgive one another in love, just as God has forgiven us.

Therefore when a Christian receives the sacrament of Penance, the sacrament of reconciliation, the sacramental absolution is the sign not only that God has forgiven him, but that the whole Christian community, and everyone in the community has also forgiven him, and has embraced him in reconciliation. The priest who absolves from sin in the sacrament of Penance does so in the name of the whole people of God, as their minister, for every sin is an offense not only against God, but against all his people. Christ, the head of his body, dispenses forgiveness and reconciliation through his body and its minister. Forgiveness and reconciliation is not simply a matter between God and the sinner, but a matter which concerns the whole body of Christ, which is hurt by every sin. Thus the whole community, by the grace and power of its head, bestows the grace of forgiveness and reconciliation through the ministry of the priest who gives absolution.

The sacrament of Penance gives us the power to go out and forgive one another. For penance is not simply a sacrament of individual forgiveness. It is a sacrament of community reconciliation. It gives the grace of the Holy Spirit to do everything that is necessary for the fullness of reconciliation.

Such reconciliation of each with all is possible only because the community is animated by God's own love poured out into the hearts of all by the Holy Spirit who is given to us. This love impels all to receive every sinner with compassion, and to work toward the fullness of forgiveness and reconciliation.

Thus the sacrament of reconciliation bears its full fruits

only when we go out in the power and grace which the sacrament has given us, and courageously seek reconciliation with our fellowmen, whether we are the ones who have offended, or the ones who have been offended. If we have offended, then we ask our brothers' forgiveness. If we have been offended, then we forgive the one who has offended us.

If I am already reconciled with God through the sacrament and am again filled with God's love by the Holy Spirit, I am the one who should take the initiative in seeking reconciliation with a sinner who has offended me. For the unreconciled sinner is still without love. For if his sin against me has been serious, it has been the rejection of love. Because the sinner is without love, he cannot come in love seeking reconciliation with me whom he has offended.

Therefore I, filled with God's own love in the sacrament of reconciliation, have to take the initiative in forgiving him and seeking him out, offering him pardon. The Father has forgiven me in Christ, and therefore I go out seeking those who have offended me, to forgive them just as Jesus sought me out and forgave me. "Blessed are the peacemakers, for they shall be called the children of God!" (Mt 5:9). The work of the sacrament of Penance and reconciliation is not complete among us until everyone in our community is fully reconciled with everyone else.

The Sacrament of Healing

So many of the sins I commit are in reaction against those who have sinned against me. Therefore I am hurt and wounded not only by the sins I myself have committed, but also by the sins committed against me, to which I have reacted. It is necessary that I be healed not only of the wounds caused in me by my own sins, but of the wounds and resentments caused in me by the sins of others against me, for many of my own sins spring from these resentments.

I must be healed of all these wounds and resentments lest they lead me to new sins after my present ones have been forgiven. I may forgive someone who has sinned against me, but the hurt he has caused me may be so deep that it still remains with me. It may easily lead me to renewed resentment and new sins, if the hurt is not thoroughly healed in the sacrament of reconciliation by the redeeming grace of Christ.

When I receive the sacrament of Penance, therefore, I should not only seek the forgiveness of sins. I should ask the priest to help me detect those wounds of which I need to be healed by the Lord's redeeming grace. I should ask him to pray that the Holy Spirit will give me light to see what needs healing, and that through the sacrament Christ will heal me.

To be healed of the hurt others have caused me by their sins, it is necessary that I recognize that the hurt and the resentment are there. It is necessary also that I forgive those who have hurt me, and renounce all resentments against them. Only then can Christ's grace completely heal me. That is why in connection with the sacrament of Penance there should always be prayer to the Holy Spirit for light to see what needs to be renounced and what needs healing.

Sometimes these hurts and resentments go back so many years in my life that I am no longer very conscious that they are there. Yet these wounds may be the cause of many of my present sins and bad relationships with my fellowmen, and also the cause of many of the sins by which I try to compensate myself for my hurts. My problems with drink or with drugs, for example, or my sins of lustful self-indulgence, may be my way of compensating myself for these long-forgotten wounds and resentments that may even go back to my childhood. By the grace of the Holy Spirit in the sacrament of reconciliation I must rediscover the cause of these wounds, and be healed of them, if I am to be freed also of the sins to which they keep leading me.

Thus one of the great fruits of the sacrament of reconciliation should be the healing of human relationships. To achieve this, the sacrament must heal me of the fears and resentments which paralyze my power to love others, and which give rise to sins against them and isolate me from them. Anyone who belongs to Christian community, and hopes for true community life, should make good use of this sacrament of Penance which is so effective in healing human relationships and restoring life to a wounded community.

The sacrament heals my human relationships by healing me of my own wounds, and by empowering me with the grace to go out and seek reconciliation with those for whom I have been isolated by sin.

Reconciliation with Individuals

Community reconciliation begins with the reconciliation of individuals who have offended and been offended. Reconciliation must take place first of all on this one-to-one basis. "If your brother sins against you," says Jesus, "go and tell him his fault, between you and him alone. If he listens to you, you have gained your brother" (Mt 18:15).

This telling our brother his fault is usually referred to as fraternal correction. It would be far better to call it fraternal reconciliation, because reconciliation is its purpose. Correction can be done in pride or vindictiveness. But reconciliation is possible only in love. In love, says Jesus, "you have gained your brother" (Mt 18:15).

When I correct another, I must take care that I do it out of love and concern for him, and not simply because his failing has been annoying or harmful to me, and a cause of resentment in me. That very resentment is an obstacle preventing healing love from flowing from me to him.

My "fraternal" correction will fail if it comes through

to him as simply my annoyance with him, or as my self-love which cannot stand him. In praying for his conversion, therefore, or in trying to correct him, I must do it only in motives of genuine love for him, in reverence for his dignity and destiny as a child of God, and in love's distress over how he is injuring himself by his sin.

Community Reconciliation Liturgies

Besides reconciliation on a one-to-one basis, liturgies of community reconciliation are very fruitful. They are extensions of the sacrament of Penance which either prepare people for the sacrament, or bring to full fruition the graces of the sacrament already received by various members of the community. In fact, the ideal way to receive the sacrament of Penance is within the context of a ceremony of total community reconciliation.

No doubt St. James is speaking of confession of sins in connection with community prayer when he writes, "Confess your sins to one another, and pray for one another that you may be healed. The prayer of a righteous man has great power in its effects" (Jas 5:16). When the sacrament of Penance is administered in the context of a community reconciliation liturgy, the whole community prays for the penitents. The sacrament of healing and reconciliation is but an effective instrument of a loving community. Only in an atmosphere of community love can it produce its richest fruits.

In a reconciliation liturgy, the community prays not only that each sinner will be forgiven by God, but also that everyone in the community will forgive each sinner. Prayer for the grace to forgive is just as important as prayer that sinners will be forgiven. For mutual giving and receiving of forgiveness are necessary for the complete community reconciliation which is the full fruit of the sacrament of Penance.

Thus, in a community penance liturgy, the whole assembly should pray that everyone present will receive the grace of a profound conversion, not only conversion from sin, but conversion toward repentant sinners. The grace of full reconciliation is possible only through such genuine metanoia, change of heart, in both the offenders and the offended.

In the liturgy of community reconciliation, individuals should have the opportunity to ask pardon of the community for faults they have committed against the community, if these faults are known by all. For example, a family community should occasionally have a ceremony of family reconciliation in which members who have been troublesome to all would have the opportunity to ask pardon of all. The same sort of ceremony should be provided occasionally in the other small groupings of the larger community.

Certainly I should confess to those whom I have injured and who know that I have injured them, whether it be an individual or a group that I have injured. Such confession and asking pardon are necessary for full reconciliation.

Moreover, every sin, even the most hidden one, really does hurt the whole body of Christ, whether everyone in the community is conscious of this hurt or not. When many of the community are not aware that my sin has hurt them, it is better that I confess, not to the community as a whole, but to the representative of the community, the priest, who reconciles me to the whole body in the name of Jesus, the head, who is present through his image, the priest. In this case I should confess also to those who know I have hurt them, asking their pardon. I confess to the whole group and ask their pardon only when the whole group knows that I am guilty of an offense against them.

Public confession of my failings when they are obnoxious and known to everyone is valuable for several reasons besides the need of reconciliation. First, my confession wins for me the sympathy and support of my community or family in my effort to conquer my failings. By confessing my weakness to my brothers and sisters I show them my goodwill in trying to do better.

But if I do not admit my weakness of which all are aware, and do not acknowledge it before the others who are suffering from it, they are inclined to think that I am not trying to overcome my failing, and they will not be well disposed toward me. They may think that I am negligent, irresponsible, unwilling to mend my ways, or even vicious, whereas in reality my heart may be crying out in its loneliness and difficulties, looking for understanding and help.

If only I would express this cry of my heart in words of confession to those with whom I live, they would embrace me in love and compassion, and would no longer judge me severely. They would no longer be tempted to think I am incorrigible, and therefore they would not avoid me as they do now. They would be more patient with my weaknesses, and would support me in my struggle to overcome them. They would be less inclined to talk about my failings behind my back. For when I have entrusted my weaknesses to their love by my confession, their love and compassion become very protective and understanding.

Entrusting our weaknesses to one another in this way by confessing to one another's love, we no longer have to bear our sinfulness in loneliness and isolation, we no longer need to hide from one another in shame. The fact that I am not alone with my burden once I have entrusted it to my brother's love makes me more courageous in struggling with my weakness, and fills me with great hope for full healing. "Bear one another's burdens," says St. Paul, "and thus you will fulfill the law of Christ" (Gal 6:2). Christ expects our community love to be very protective of its weak members, healing them in its compassionate love.

Protective Covenant Love

By its very nature, Christian covenant love is protective of the weak and sinful, for Christ shed the blood of the covenant for all. Covenant love is characterized by family loyalty. Even in the Old Testament, we have seen, the covenant love uniting God's people was essentially a family love, for in making the covenant, God accepted the people as his family. He described his covenant relationship with them in the terms which expressed the traditional Hebrew family ideals. The steadfast love and faithfulness binding God's family together included not simply affection and kindness, but also an undying loyalty to one another. This unshakable loyalty is the foundation of the wonderful trust and confidence in one another without which happy life is not possible.

Family loyalty of its very nature is impelled to be protective even of the wayward members of the family, loyally defending even these against attacks. Covenant love extends this loyalty and protectiveness to every member of the Christian community. Christian covenant love, poured out into our hearts by the Holy Spirit given to us in Christ's blood, protects even the sinners among us. It compassionately seeks to correct them, is ever ready to forgive them, and joyfully receives them back when they confess their sins. Correlative with the sinner's responsibility to repent and seek reconciliation is the community's responsibility to seek him out and receive him back, in the covenant loyalty which binds us together irrevocably in the new covenant in Christ's blood.

If we have faith and hope in God's forgiving love, we must have faith and hope in one another's forgiving love. In fact, the community's loving forgiveness makes it possible for us to believe in God's forgiveness. God's own love and forgiveness are operative and manifest in the community's forgiveness. When someone comes to confess his failings and to ask forgiveness, the community experiences God's own compassionate heart at work in itself, and receives the sinner with joy.

Thus, the confession of sins to the community, or to the priest who is the representative of the community, is a confession of our faith and trust in our brothers and sisters as Christians, endowed with the Lord's own compassion and readiness to forgive. If Christians lived true to the nature of their covenant family bond, confession of their sins to one another could easily become a normal thing.

Without confession and reconciliation, we split farther apart from one another, and become ever more isolated. Lacking in loving loyalty, we lose trust in one another, and become unable to believe in love. Without easy opportunity for confession and quick reconciliation, community quickly deteriorates, and divisions become steadily deeper and harder to heal.

But when Christian convenant love develops the aspect of family loyalty to one another, and is very protective even of the sinful and of those struggling with their weaknesses, community grows strong, and enjoys a wonderful healing power within it, because of the vitality of its loyal love for all its members.

Community in the Lord is essentially a community of daily forgiveness and reconciliation. In the Lord's Prayer we ask the Father: Give us this day not only our daily bread, but also the forgiveness of our sins. Forgive us this day our trespasses, as we forgive this day those who trespass against us.

Part 6

*Community and the
Charismatic Graces*

Chapter 19

Charismatic Graces Build Community

Charismatic graces are essential for building up Christian community, and have always been operative wherever there has been true community in the Lord. The Lord in person builds his community through the workings of these graces.

St. Paul defines the charismatic graces as "manifestations of the Spirit for the common good" (1 Cor 12:7). Their purpose is building up the body of Christ. Thus they differ from the sanctifying graces, whose purpose is to bring each individual to the fullness of his personal holiness.

Through sanctifying grace, the Christian enters into the very life of the three divine Persons, for he is born of water and the Holy Spirit as an adopted child of God in Jesus, the Son of God. In the Son he enters into direct relationship with the Father, in the love poured out into his heart by the Holy Spirit who is given to him.

The sanctifying graces include the seven gifts of the Holy Spirit: wisdom, understanding, knowledge, counsel, fortitude, piety and fear of the Lord. Through the seven kinds of inspiration granted through these gifts, the Spirit leads the individual Christian to the full perfection of his sharing in the life of the Holy Trinity. Infused contemplation, for example, through which a person directly experiences the God who dwells within him, is granted through the working of the gifts of wisdom and understanding.

The sanctifying graces have been treated in great detail in multitudes of spiritual writings through the centuries. Until recent years, however, not a great deal has been written about the charismatic graces, the graces by which the Lord builds up his body, the community.

The term "charismatic grace" or "charism" has usually been used with too restricted a meaning. Here we are using the term in the broader meaning which St. Paul gives it in First Corinthians.

The Corinthians, it seems, had been disputing about the relative value of the different charismatic graces, and valued some of them, such as speaking in tongues, more highly than others. In his teaching in response to these disputes, Paul deliberately lumps all the charismatic graces together, and to describe them uses four different words as though these four words were synonyms. Each of the words is used to describe all the graces given by the Spirit for building up the community. Each of the words brings out a different characteristic of one same reality:

"Now concerning spiritual gifts (*pneumata*). . . . There are varieties of gifts (*charismata*), but the same *Spirit;* and there are varieties of service (*diakonia*), but the same *Lord;* and there are varieties of working (*energemata*), but it is the same *God* who inspires them all in every one" (1 Cor 12:1, 4-6).

In this passage, "gifts," "services," "workings" are but different words for the "pneumata," the "inspirations" or spiritual gifts which build up the body of Christ. And "Spirit," "Lord," "God" are the three divine Persons, the one source of all the gifts. All the gifts have their origin then in the one Holy Trinity, all of them work together as a unity toward one purpose: to bring us all into communion with the Holy Trinity, in the one body of Christ.

First, Paul calls all the gifts *pneumata* (12:1). Though this word is usually translated "spiritual gifts," it means "spirits." Paul personifies the gifts as "spirits" because "it is the same God who *inspires* them all in every one" (12:6), and all of them are manifestations of the Holy Spirit for building up the community (12:7).

Paul also calls all the charisms "workings," *energemata,* because the one same God works powerfully in all of them. And he calls them *diakonia,* "ministries" or "services," because all of them serve the common good of the body of Christ. He calls all of them *charismata,* "gifts," because all of them are the effect of grace freely given by God.

The apostle makes clear that he wishes to apply the term *charismata* to all the gifts which build up the body, because he uses this word in opening and in closing his whole treatment of the subject (1 Cor 12:4, 31). The word is used also in speaking of those ministries whose powers are conferred by ordination, the laying on of hands (1 Tm 1:14; 2 Tm 1:16). Thus, the scriptures include the hierarchical functions of bishops, priests and deacons among the charismatic graces, the graces whose purpose is the building up of Christian community.

Because of the marvelous unity in the origin, working, and purpose of the charismatic graces, no one need be upset that he does not have this charism or that one. God distributes them to each according to his own will (Eph 4:7), giving this grace to one, that gift to another. Some charisms, such as word gifts, may seem more glamorous than others. But all the graces are important, for all are necessary services rendered to the whole body. Even the most hidden services in the community help build up the body, and are charismatic to the extent that they are inspired by the love poured out into our hearts by the Holy Spirit.

Charisms Always Working

Charismatic graces, we said, have always been at work wherever the life of the Christian community has been vigorous. But until very recently we did not even think of most of these graces as charisms, because we had restricted the meaning of that word too much. The charismatic reality was there, however, even when we did not give it the name. Even when we did not recognize the reality for what it is, we always did take it for granted as a normal part of vigorous Christian living.

Thus, for example, charismatic graces have always been operative in Christian homes where fathers and mothers used the gifts of teaching, encouragement, admonition, and the like. From time immemorial God has spoken to us through the mouths of little children. How often in astonishment at this we have acknowledged it, saying, "Out of the mouths of babes and sucklings you have brought perfect praise" (Mt 21:16). Charismatic graces have been operative in the Christian community whenever men and women carried out self-giving service of the sinful, the ignorant, the poor, the sick, the needy. For centuries religious men and women have been using the teaching charisms in a powerful way in our Christian schools. Laywomen like Catherine of Siena, Elizabeth of Hungary, Frances of Rome, Bridget of Sweden exerted a profound charismatic influence on great numbers of people. Charismatic statesmen like St. Louis of France, St. Stephen of Hungary, St. Henry of Germany, brought about Christian government in their times and worked for a Christian social order. Charismatic leaders like Dominic and Francis brought forth great religious orders, in which multitudes of charismatic graces were exercised in preaching, in educational work, in social work; the care of the needy, the orphaned, the aged, the imprisoned, the sick and the sinful.

Charisms have always been there. We simply took them for granted and had no name for them, until these recent times when the charity of men has grown so cold that God has had to intervene with a powerful new display of the more striking charisms, such as tongues and singing in the Spirit, to alert us once again to the fact that he wants to do great things in our times, just as he had done in past centuries.

Once again in these days we are expecting God to act in this charismatic way. There is no other way to full community in the Lord, for "unless the Lord build the house" through graces like these, "they labor in vain who strive to build it" (Ps 127:1). Since the Lord wills Christian community, we should expect him to pour out these graces without which it cannot exist.

One of the distinctive marks of the contemporary charismatic renewal is the conviction that the Lord *will* do these things; and therefore he *can* do them because we are open to these graces in expectant faith and hope; the Lord grants us as much as we expect when we are concerned for his glory and the good of our fellowmen.

Charisms as Communication and Service

Community is impossible without self-giving love, and this love has to be expressed in communication and service. The charismatic graces are all graces of communication and service, through which the Holy Spirit brings God's people together as one body in the Lord.

All the charisms involve communication, and all of them are services. Sometimes in the scriptures, however, the word "service" is restricted to those forms of living exchange which are not "word gifts." Peter writes, for example, "As each has received a gift, employ it for one another, as good stewards of God's varied grace; whoever speaks, as one who utters oracles of God; whoever renders service, as one who renders it by the strength which God supplies" (1 Pt 4:11).

As graces of communication and service, charisms are graces of listening and response, of hearing the Lord and carrying out his word, of being attentive to one another in love and responding in love, of being alert to needs and responding to these needs.

In some of the charisms, the word gifts, direct communication is established between the Lord and his people. Besides preaching and teaching, other word gifts, such as prophecy, the words of wisdom and the words of knowledge, are integral parts of the Church's ministry of the word. This ministry functions not only in the official liturgy, but also in other forms of community prayer, in various kinds of evangelism, and in various educational situations.

The other charisms, such as the services of love and mercy, also have their elements of communication. Services presuppose communication among God's people: loving attentiveness to one another, love's ability to notice needs and respond to them, love's listening to what cries out in the very being of others. The services rendered in response to these needs are charismatic to the extent that they are inspired by the love poured out into our hearts by the Holy Spirit, the love which opens our hearts to listen, to understand, and to respond with compassionate and generous self-giving. God's own love and presence is thus manifest through these charismatic services, which are like an eloquent nonverbal communication from God to his people.

Charisms such as leadership, administration, discernment also require a listening, understanding, loving heart which is always in full communication with those who are subject to this leadership and government.

If in recent times the charismatic effects have not been

very manifest in our pastoral care, in our schools, in our preaching, in our works of mercy, in caring for the sick, the poor, the needy, perhaps it is because we have failed to be in living communication with God and with one another in love's attentiveness.

Even the lowliest of services rendered in the Christian community, such as cleaning floors or washing dishes, when they are manifestations of love, are manifestations of Christ and his Spirit in our midst, and thus have the charismatic quality. It is not so much the service itself which manifests the Lord, but the love and Spirit expressed in the service.

Love can even turn one's whole person into a kind of charismatic grace for the upbuilding of the body. The more radical and complete is my gift of self in love to the Lord and to his body, the more effectively the Holy Spirit can use me in charismatic services. Thus, my gift of self in faith and love is presupposed to all my charismatic graces. For this reason, the most fundamental charismatic service I render is the gift of my whole person to the service of the Lord and his body in love's total availability.

Through such love, my whole person becomes a kind of living charism, a grace upbuilding the body of the Lord. For the Lord himself becomes vividly manifest in me. Others sense the presence of God in my peace and joy and love. I bring peace and comfort and courage to them by my presence as a loving person, by my patient, attentive, listening heart, by the sincerity of my self-giving to the Lord and his people, by my fullness of presence in loving-kindness to all who need me. By my quiet, peaceful trust in God, my whole being cries out peace and light, courage and love, joy and inspiration.

Such a loving, charismatic presence is greater than a multitude of other charisms in a person who is less loving. For example, a beginner in Christian living, one who is not yet too profound or experienced in deep love for his fellowmen, can nonetheless be used by the Lord in gifts such as prophecy, preaching, teaching, even when his love is not yet perfect. But through utter and total availability in perfect love, another person may be building up the body of Christ in a quiet powerful way without the aid of the more striking charisms such as prophecy or healing. The joy and peace of God shining forth in his whole person can be a presence of God drawing many others to the Lord, and bringing them the peace and calm necessary for full joy in the Lord.

The total gift of myself to the service of the body in love is thus the greatest charismatic service I can render. The totality of my gift of self is manifest in my Christian poverty, in which I keep nothing for myself, not even myself, but give all that I am and all that I have in total availability to others in love. "Now the company of those who believed were of one heart and soul, and no one said that any of the things which he possessed was his own, but they had everything in common" (Acts 4:32). In Christian community, we share all that we have and all that we are. The availability of all my possessions, all my talents, all my powers and energies to those who are in need, presupposes the availability of my very person to my brothers and sisters in the Lord. Evangelical poverty, or the consecration of all that I am and have to the good of the Body of Christ, surrenders me totally to the Lord in "charismatic openness" to him, to be used in whatever way he sees fit to use me.

The same things are true in an even more striking way of consecrated celibacy, which, like poverty, is charismatic openness to the Lord: It is the total surrender of my whole person to the Lord to be used by him as a kind of living charismatic grace for the benefit of the whole body. Espoused directly to the divine Bridegroom, the celibate exists exclusively for the Lord and his work of universal love. The total dying to self entailed by celibacy makes the celibate a living sacrifice offered for the good of the whole body of Christ, and thus a kind of living charismatic grace.

All the charisms, then, are "graces" for they are all gifts of God's own love given to us in Christ through the Holy Spirit. They are all "spirits," because all are inspired by the Holy Spirit and the generous love which he pours out into our hearts. All of them are "services," for all respond to needs. All of them are "ministries," for in their workings the Lord himself uses us as his ministers, and works through our love. All are "workings," for in them the God of power himself is present and acting.

Through these workings we are all knit together in one body in loving communion and exchange. "Living the truth in love, we are to grow up in every way into him who is the head, into Christ, from whom the whole body, joined and knit together by every joint with which it is supplied, when each part is working properly, makes bodily growth and upbuilds itself in love" (Eph 4:15-16).

Chapter 20

The Charism of Headship

Among the charisms of the Christian community, St. Paul lists leadership and government. "He who rules should exercise his authority with care" (Rm 12:8 *NAB*). If you are a leader, exert yourself to lead" (Rm 12:8 *NEB*). "God has appointed in the church first apostles, second prophets, third teachers, then . . . administrators. . ." (1 Cor 12:28).

The charisms of administration and leadership are ways of serving in building up the body of Christ. They are a participation in the Lord's own leadership and headship over his body, the Church.

Sometimes this grace of headship is bestowed through the laying on of hands in the sacrament of ordination to the office of bishop, priest, or deacon. The sacrament of Orders configures the ordained men to Christ in such a way that they are image and presence of Christ, precisely as head of the whole Church. For priests and deacons participate in the bishop's leadership over the whole flock, and exercise the bishop's headship in the local churches entrusted to them.

Sometimes headship is bestowed through a special charismatic grace distinct from Holy Orders. Through this grace the Lord selects a leader for a lesser community which the Lord himself is building within the larger community; for example, a religious congregation within the total community of the Church, or a charismatic community within a diocese or a parish. Such charismatic graces of headship, as distinct from Holy Orders, are a more limited sharing in the headship of Christ than is the headship conferred by Orders, for they are restricted to headship only over a smaller community within the larger community of the Church.

Sometimes the charism of headship is an integral part of a vocation, such as that of a father of a family, who, in the Lord's plan, is head of the family. Heads of families and of households have a limited sharing in Christ's headship, for they are image and presence of Christ the Head only over their own family or household.

Sometimes headship is the special charism of spiritual direction of few or many individuals within any of the larger communities which we have mentioned.

Leadership in the Spirit

In describing the functions of a head or spiritual shepherd, we shall limit ourselves to considering only certain general principles which apply to all who have the charism of leadership, whether it be pope, bishop, priest, head of religious community, spiritual director, elder in a charismatic community, head of a household, or head of a family.

Since headship is a grace from God, a gift of the Lord to his people, it brings a special presence of the Holy Spirit in the head. Because each head in his own way shares in and exercises the Lord's own headship over his body, like the Lord himself, each head follows the Spirit's lead. In his gospel, St. Luke shows how the Lord Jesus, the head of the Church, always followed the Holy Spirit; in the Acts, Luke shows how the whole Church, and each one in it, is led by the same Holy Spirit:

When Jesus had been baptized and was praying, the Holy Spirit descended upon him. . . (Lk 3:22). Full of the Holy Spirit, Jesus returned from the Jordan, and was led by the Spirit for forty days in the wilderness (4:1). He returned in the power of the Spirit into Galilee (4:14). He came to Nazareth. . . . He opened the book and found the place where it was written, "The Spirit of the Lord is upon me" (4:18). He thrilled with joy in the Holy Spirit (10:21).

The gospels show how Jesus prayed before each new step in his ministry (Mk 1:38; Lk 3:21; 6:12; 9:18; 9:28-31; 18:1; 22:32; Jn 17). Only through submission to God through prayer are we fully open to the Spirit's leadership.

In the following pages, everything we shall say about heads of communities applies also to heads of lesser groups, such as fathers of families, leaders of households, spiritual directors.

The Spirit in Each

The special presence of the Holy Spirit in the head of a community is frustrated if the head disregards the Spirit's presence in the community as a whole and in each person in the community. Like Solomon, every leader needs "a listening heart" (1 Kgs 3:9), to listen to God and to each person whom God has entrusted to his leadership. He needs a discerning heart, to distinguish the good from the evil in the hearts of all those in his care. He must exercise the charism of "testing the spirit" (cf. 1 Thes 5:19-22).

For though leadership is directed to the common good of the whole body, it achieves this common good only by promoting the maximum good of each member of the body in its relationship to the whole. Therefore in exercising his authority, the leader's first care is to be attentive to the Holy Spirit who speaks in each person under his headship.

Listening to the Spirit working in everyone in his charge, his basic question in regard to each person is always: "What does the Lord want of this person? Where is the Spirit leading him?"

The general answer to this question is always the same: The Lord wants each person to be his true self, the person the Lord is calling him to be, the self the Spirit is leading him to be.

Therefore the unique dignity of each individual person in the community must always be a prime consideration of every leader. For the leader carries on the work of Jesus, the Good Shepherd, who calls each of his sheep by name. The distinctive name of each signifies the distinctive person he is called to be. Each one is called to his unique place in the Lord's body, which he can fill only by being the person the Lord wants him to be.

Even though each one's vocation is a call to a role in the Lord's body, it is first of all a call to a direct personal relationship with the Lord himself, who is the "bridegroom" not only of the whole body, but also of each individual Christian. This call of each to personal intimacy with the Lord is always primary, and is to be respected above all else by anyone exercising leadership in the body. The leader has to be like John the Baptist, pointing only to the Lord, saying, "He must increase, I must decrease" (Jn 3:30).

No leader, or father, or mother, ever owns the persons in their charge. Everyone under the care of a head must always be reverenced as a son or daughter of God, who belongs first of all to the Lord, to be led by the Lord's own Spirit.

In giving direction, then, the leader's aim must always be to show each person in his charge how to discern the Spirit's leadings and to follow him lovingly, how to hear the bridegroom's voice (Jn 3:29), the Good Shepherd's call (Jn 10:3), and thus become the person the Lord meant him to be.

Respect for each individual as a unique person, son of God and bride of Christ in the Spirit, is basic even to direction of the body as a whole. For each one's contribution to the building of the body is in proportion to how completely he develops as the unique person the Lord is calling him to be. It is only within the body, of course, and in relationship with all the other persons in it, that each one achieves his own full dignity and personhood.

Since the Spirit speaks to each person who is under the leader's care, the leader's aim, then, is always to show each person how to surrender to the Lord and his Spirit. Only to the extent that each one is directly submissive to the Lord himself is he useful to the body. The leader helps each person discover his true vocation and its charisms, and to fulfill his responsibilities within the body.

Responsible Submission to Leadership

Always, the leader aims for the maximum personal maturity of each one under his headship. He inspires each one to assume full responsibility for his own decisions and actions. Each one must seek, find, accept and fulfill his unique personal role in the body, thus becoming to the full the person the Lord calls him to be. The leader "decreases" like John the Baptist as the one he directs more and more fully follows the Holy Spirit.

For the goal of all Christian leadership and spiritual direction is to show each person how to let the Holy Spirit be his director. The leader helps each to discern the Spirit in his own life, and to make personal decisions in mature responsibility. The goal of all direction is full freedom in the Spirit for the one directed, so that the one directed more and more assumes full responsibility for his personal life and for his role in the body of Christ.

Parents, too, in directing their children, must aim at forming their children to assume ever greater personal responsibility for their conduct and actions. Every director, of course, and above all parents, must also know how to be patient, and not expect maturity to come without a long process of growth. Some parents make the mistake of expecting their children to be perfect before the children could possibly have grown to perfection, and, by their perfectionistic demands, expose the children to the danger of utter discouragement in the face of these unreasonable demands.

Even among adults, there are still stages of growth toward greater maturity in the Spirit, and the community and its leaders lovingly know how to accept people where they are.

The more mature each person is in actively accepting and fulfilling his responsibilities, the more valuable he is to the whole body, and the better the material the leader has to work with in directing all the members to building up the whole body.

This, then, is a cardinal principle of Christian leadership: Respect and safeguard first of all each one's personal dignity and freedom, and his loving submission directly to the Lord and his Spirit.

Because Christian leadership inspires full maturity and personal responsibility in those who are led, it is obvious that submission to such leadership is never passive surrender or abdication of responsibility. On the contrary, it is active and responsible cooperation with the leader for the good of everyone concerned.

The full maturity of the individual and his freedom in the Spirit does not exclude his seeking direction from the head and from following his directions. One point of maturity, indeed, is the ability to follow leadership. Effective authority and submission to authority are essential for true community, and community is impossible without them.

In matters of each one's personal life, the leader only counsels and lets the person under his leadership make the decisions. But in matters which concern the whole community, after listening to the Spirit speaking through each member of the community, the leader makes the decisions, in the light of the Spirit's special presence in him as leader.

Those who are under leadership are submissive to the Holy Spirit working in the leader, while the leader is submissive to the Holy Spirit working in those whom he leads. This twofold submission to the Spirit by head and members is for the good of the whole body and of each person in the body.

How the Spirit Speaks

Since the leader reverences each person as one whom the Spirit leads, one to whom the Spirit speaks, in making decisions for the whole body the leader takes into consideration what the Spirit is saying to the individual members of the body, and helps each to be his true self within the common good of the whole.

The Spirit speaks to the individual persons in the body in a variety of ways: in their consciences, in their prayer, in their experienced needs, in the events making up their lives, in the talents and gifts the Lord has given them to be developed, in the special attractions of grace which he plants in them, in the needs of the community to which he calls them by this grace. The leader must not stifle the Spirit working in a person by ignoring any of these ways in which the Lord reveals his will for the person.

In the light of what the Spirit is doing in the whole body, then, the leader discerns and judges all that the Spirit is doing in the individual, remembering always that each person fulfills his truest role in the body by being the person the Lord is leading him to be. What the Spirit is doing in the whole body is a clue as to what he is doing in each member, just as what he is doing in each member is a clue to what he wants to do in the whole body, and how he wants this person to be a living grace for the whole body.

"Onesimus": Useful in the Lord

Because the leader always respects each individual's personal dignity and freedom in the Spirit, no one in the community is ever "used" or treated as though he were expendable for the common good.

Yet the scriptures speak of us all as "useful in the Lord" (Phlm 20). The very words "minister" and "ministry" indicate that the Lord uses the members of his body in carrying on his own work. A minister is a living instrument used by another person. Precisely because his ministers are persons, however, the Lord uses them only to the extent that they lovingly and willingly give themselves to his service in full freedom.

This is evident in Paul's letter to Philemon. Paul considers both Philemon and his slave Onesimus useful to him in carrying out his apostolic work. The name Onesimus means "useful," and throughout the letter Paul keeps making wordplays on this name. "I want to make you 'useful' to me in the Lord," he says to Philemon (20). The whole letter explains how.

Paul had wished to keep Philemon's slave Onesimus with him, so that Philemon would be useful to him through his useful slave. "I had wanted to keep him with me, that he might serve in your place while I am in prison for the gospel" (13). However, Paul refuses to "use" Onesimus, for, like Christ, he wants only a willing service given in the fullness of love. Onesimus is willing, but is Philemon, his owner, willing? Therefore, Paul continues: "But I preferred to do nothing without your consent, in order that your goodness might not be by compulsion, but of your own free will" (14); "I prefer to appeal in the name of love" (9).

Paul presents his appeal to Philemon's love between two references to the refreshing power of that love. "I have derived much joy and comfort from your love, my brother, because the hearts of God's people have been refreshed through you" (7). Be useful to me by sending Useful back to me in the fullness of your love! "Refresh my heart in Christ!" (20).

"Formerly he was useless to you" (when he was rebellious and ran away), "but now he is useful to you and to me in the Lord" (11). For he is now a brother in the Lord: "It may be that he was parted from you for a short time so that you might have him back for all time. For now he is not just a slave, but much more than a slave: he is a dear brother in Christ. How much he means to me! And how much more he will mean to you, both as a slave and as a brother in the Lord!" (16-17).

As a brother in the Lord, he will now serve you, and me, in joyous and willing love. You will receive him in love, you will send him back to me in love, he will come to me in love.

Though Paul refuses to "use" Onesimus, he gratefully welcomes Philemon's and Onesimus's loving gift of their usefulness. The only truly Christian service is willing service of the Lord, to whom we give ourselves completely in love. Hence, in exhorting submission to leadership, Paul always calls it submission to the Lord: "Wives, be subject to your husbands as to the Lord" (Eph 5:22). "Children, obey your parents in the Lord" (6:1). "Slaves, be obedient to your masters . . . in singleheartedness as to Christ, . . . rendering service with a good will as to the Lord" (6:5-7).

Like Paul, Christian leaders strive to inspire each one's loving gift of self to the Lord, each one's self-sacrifice in following the Spirit's lead and doing the Lord's will. The leader inspires this not simply by words of exhortation, but especially by his own loving self-giving in serving those in his charge. Like the Good Shepherd, he lays down his life for the sheep.

For we are "useful in the Lord" only to the degree that our gift of self to the Lord is wholehearted. We are useless to the extent that we are self-seeking in our service, and hold back in selfishness.

That is why in raising up charismatic communities and wishing to have people who are useful in forwarding his work, the Lord begins by inspiring in them hearty praise of God. In praising the Lord with all their hearts, they forget themselves, and focus totally on the Lord and on his loving purposes. In full freedom of Spirit, they surrender to him in wholehearted love. Experience shows that where there is hearty praise of God in community, self-surrender to the Lord follows, and the charismatic graces are poured out abundantly. Only to the extent that we have surrendered directly to the Lord in love are we useful to his body, the community of love.

No one is ever "used" in the community of love. All are brothers and sisters in the Lord, and each one lovingly, willingly, joyously gives himself in generous service.

Community Is People Growing

The goal of leadership, we said, is to bring each of the persons led to full personal responsibility and maturity in the Spirit. But in community we should never forget that persons reach maturity only through a process of growing together.

Just as "friendship is two people growing,"[1] so commu-

1. This is the title of a chapter in *Friendship in the Lord*. Practically all that is said in that book about the relationships of friends applies to all relationships in community.

nity is many people growing together, and there are many growing pains. People go through many different stages in their process of growth, and we must lovingly accept them at whatever stage of growth they are.

One of the big problems in community, and especially religious communities, is that we do not allow people to go through stages of growth. We expect them to be perfect from the beginning! This in spite of the ancient tradition, going back at least to St. Benedict, that religious community is not the abode of people at the summit of perfection, but is a school of perfection. This is true of all Christian community. We are a pilgrim church still on the way home to our Father, a church of sinners still in process of being redeemed.

When the requirements of community are too exacting, and no allowance is made for human weakness and human immaturity, the weak and the immature find it exceedingly difficult to accept themselves as they are, still involved in problems of growth. They succumb to discouragement and self-condemnation when they cannot meet the standards set up by the self-righteous in the community.

Many of us are immature because we have not had time or opportunuity to grow, or were retarded by the failure of others to provide the loving atmosphere necessary for human and spiritual growth. We must therefore be patient with one another. If we do not allow one another the time and the opportunity to mature, we force our weaker brothers and sisters to withdraw within themselves, broken in spirit, because they cannot meet our demanding standards.

A person who knows he is imperfect and admits it humbly, and is trying to grow, is not to be nagged into "perfection," but is to be received patiently with understanding, and supported with love and compassion.

When it is obvious, of course, that no growth is taking

place, because of the negligence, indifference, or self-indulgence of the immature, they have to be confronted by the community or by their leaders, and made to face the truth about themselves. Just as two friends must face the truth about each other,[2] so must a community as community face its problems, whether these be the lack of growth in individuals, or problems of human relationships, or problems of negligence by the community as a whole, or whatever the problems may be. The life of a community will rapidly deteriorate if its problems are not faced together.

The leader of a community has the responsibility of making his community face the issues and come to community decisions, instead of trying to sweep problems under the rug.

---

2. *Friendship in the Lord,* pp. 72-73.

Chapter 21

The Charisms and the Uncreated Grace

Charismatic Graces and the Sacraments

The charismatic graces are necessary for the full fruitfulness of the seven sacraments instituted by Christ. This will be evident from a brief analysis of the respective roles of sacraments and charisms in building up the Lord's body.

We usually define the charismatic graces as manifestations of the Spirit working to build up the body. But more fundamentally than through the charisms, it is through the sacraments that the Lord builds up his body through the working of his Spirit, and the charismatic workings simply bring to completion what the sacraments begin.

In the sacrament of Baptism, in which we are born again in water by the power of the Holy Spirit (Jn 3:5), we enter directly into the Lord himself, for, says Paul, we are "baptized into Christ Jesus" (Rm 6:3). By being baptized into the Lord, we enter into his body, the Church. It is not because we are in the Church that we are in the Lord, it is because we are in the Lord that we are in the Church. We are in the body of Christ, the community, only because in the Spirit we are united directly to the Lord in person.

Eucharistic communion, too, is direct union with the personal body of the risen Lord. "The bread which we break, is it not a participation in the body of Christ? Because there is one bread, we who are many are one body, for we all partake of the one bread" (1 Cor 10:16-17). Paul is saying clearly in these words that we are the body of Christ, the community, only because we are united with his personal body, the body which was crucified and is now living forevermore, and which is given to us in the Eucharist.

Body, in Paul's language, means the whole living person. Baptized into Christ, and eating his body in the Eucharist, each of us is united directly with the very person of the risen Lord, and all of us together, as one body with him, are one mystical person with him.

Only because of our direct union with the Lord do we have union with each other. "All of us in union with Christ form one body; and as parts of it we belong to each other" (Rm 12:5). Thus, it is because we are in the Lord that we are church and community. Community in the Lord results only from this direct personal union of each with the Lord.

All the charismatic graces are rooted in the sacrament of Baptism, in which, through the Spirit, we become one body with Christ. "It was in one Spirit that all of us, whether Jew or Greek, slave or free, were baptized into one body, and all of us have been given to drink of the one Spirit" (1 Cor 12:13). Paul says this in the midst of his consideration of the charismatic graces, and thus puts them into proper relationship with Baptism. Through the working of the Holy Spirit we are baptized into the body of the Lord, and in consequence of this the Holy Spirit continues and completes the work of building up the body through the functioning of the charisms.

The body, the community, is founded upon the sacraments in which we are directly built upon the Lord and united with his very Person. But it is the charisms, in a way, which keep the body fully alive by keeping its mem-

bers fully in communion and mutual exchange with the
Lord and with one another. The charisms, as it were, stir
up the grace which is in us through the various sacraments,
bringing the life which is in each of us into full vital inter-
play with the life which is in Christ the Head and is in the
other members of the body.

In what follows we shall see that the charisms build the
body into a living temple of the Lord, in the sense that they
vitalize it for the worship of the Lord who dwells in it in
person, in intimate communion with his people.

The Charisms and Focus on the Lord

The charismatic graces bring us to the Lord in person, in
whom we have direct access to the Father in the one Holy
Spirit (Eph 2:18).

Thus, the various charisms exercised in the ministry of
the word, such as preaching, teaching, prophecy, word of
wisdom, either call us to the Lord for the first time, or con-
vert us to him again if we have drifted away, or focus our
love and attention ever more fully upon him. The use of
the charisms is directed toward building up and deepening
the faith of Christians, and this faith is summed up in the
acclamation, "Jesus Christ is Lord!" (Phil 2:11).

Therefore when St. Paul prefaces his treatment of the
charisms by saying, "No one can say, 'Jesus is Lord!' except
in the Holy Spirit" (1 Cor 12:3), he is declaring that the
whole purpose of all the charisms is to bring us in one body
directly to the person of the Lord. The Lord present in
person is the focus of all the charisms. They all point to
him and call for submission to him in the one body.

Faith itself is a total consecration of one's person to the
Lord, so that he may use us for his purposes of love. The
more completely a person is surrendered to the Lord in
lively faith, the more effectively the Lord can use him
through the charismatic graces for the common good of the

body. The Lord consecrates those who use the charisms to the service of the whole body.

The goal of all this service is to bring God's people into direct communion with the Lord in the unity of the community. The charisms flow from the Lord through his Holy Spirit, and bring the united community directly to his person. The living Christian dwells immediately in Christ and Christ dwells immediately in him: "I live, now not I, but Christ lives in me" (Gal 2:20). And in Christ, the Christian is in immediate communion with the Father in the Holy Spirit. "If anyone loves me, he will keep my word, and my Father will love him, and we will come to him, and make our home with him" (Jn 14:23).

Thus, communion with the Lord is communion with the three divine Persons. In Christ, we are at home with the Holy Trinity. The deepest essence of the life in the Spirit is not the Spirit's activity in building up the body through the charismatic graces, but is the very life which is lived in that body: our sharing in the inner life of the Holy Trinity.

This will be more evident if we consider more closely the nature of the body which the Spirit is building up through the charismatic graces. The body of Christ, the Christian community, is the dwelling place of the Holy Trinity. It is the living temple where God's presence is manifested and appreciated. "Christ Jesus himself is the cornerstone in whom the whole structure is joined together and grows into a holy temple in the Lord, in whom you also are built into it, for a dwelling place for God in the Spirit" (Eph 2:22).

The Uncreated Grace

Thus, the charismatic graces are secondary graces, subordinate to an infinitely greater grace, the uncreated grace. The uncreated grace is God's gift of himself directly to his people. Only God himself is uncreated; everything else has been created by him. All other graces and charisms are created effects and manifestations of the uncreated grace, God's presence in his people. All other graces impel and direct up toward that presence. Everything else that the Holy Spirit does among us, including the charismatic graces, works toward bringing God's people into ever more direct and intimate communion with the three divine Persons. "They who are led by the Spirit are the children of God" (Rm 8:14), living in Christ in intimate union with the Father and in communion with one another.

Paul speaks of the charisms as "manifestations of the Spirit" (1 Cor 12:7). As manifestations, they are in the category of sign. But a sign always points to a deeper reality. The signs will pass away, the reality will remain forever. The reality is the uncreated grace, the Christian's life in the Holy Trinity which he is already living in a hidden way. "Your life is hidden with Christ in God. But when Christ your life appears, then you also will appear with him in glory" (Col 3:3).

When the reality of God's life in us is fully revealed, there will be no more need for the signs. "Prophecies will cease, tongues will be silent, knowledge will pass away. Our knowledge is imperfect and our prophesying is imperfect. When the perfect comes the imperfect will pass away. . . . There are in the end three things that last: faith, hope and love, and the greatest of these is love" (1 Cor 13:8-13).

Faith, hope and love remain day and night throughout the life of the fervent Christian. Charisms come and go as passing graces whose purposes are to stir up ardent faith, hope and love. In active faith, hope and love, we have direct communion in the life of the three divine Persons.

While this full reality is still hidden in the darkness of faith, the charisms, as signs and graces impelling toward it, serve the purpose of building up faith in the Lord, truly present in the midst of his people. His people acclaim him, "Jesus is Lord!" not simply in words of praise, but more eloquently still in the fruit of that praise: the total surrender of self directly to the Person of the Lord, that he might dwell in each of us and in all of us together, with the fullness of his own Trinitarian life.

How foolish it would be to concentrate on the signs and miss the reality! How shortsighted to set one's heart so firmly on having this charism or that charism that one misses the great reality of which the charisms are only the signs and instruments: the reality of God's indwelling in our hearts. The life hidden with Christ in God is the essential grace, and can be very profound indeed in persons who have none of the more striking charisms, but who are exercising more humble charisms of service. It is not necessary to have the extraordinary charisms in order to live fervently the full life in the Spirit.

We do not mean to undervalue the charismatic graces. Recent experience in the Church has been manifesting how wonderfully powerful these gifts are in bringing people directly to the Lord and alerting them to his presence. But there are always those persons who hold on so tightly to one of the lesser gifts, such as a charism, a vision, a supernatural word, or some mystical phenomenon, that they are not open to receive the full reality toward which all these graces point: the indwelling God, who gives his very self in the uncreated grace. The charisms and the mystical phenomena are of value only to the extent that they bring us more deeply into the full reality of intimacy with the Holy Trinity.

The life in the Spirit is not the charisms. The charisms are manifestations and instruments of the life in the Spirit. Life in the Spirit in its deepest essence is our participation in the life of the three divine Persons. "All who are led by the Spirit of God are sons of God" (Rm 8:14). Surrender to the Lord in lively faith, hope and love opens us ever more fully to the sanctifying gifts of the Spirit, those gifts through which we are so surrendered to the Holy Spirit that he can deepen in us God's own life and bring us ever more intimately into the inner life of the Holy Trinity. Among the sanctifying gifts, we said, are wisdom and understanding, through which we directly experience God in infused contemplation.

This life in the Trinity, still hidden in our hearts, is expressed outwardly in the body of Christ, the Christian community. The charisms, building up the body and manifesting its life, are therefore necessary until the full revelation of the "life now hidden with Christ in God" (Col 3:3).

Living Temple

All the charisms, we said, flow from the three divine Persons and lead us to them, who are the uncreated grace given to us to be enjoyed and appreciated.

Our appreciation and enjoyment of the three divine Persons do not have to wait till the next life. God is already present and manifest in his temple on earth, the body of Christ. Much of his self-manifestation in this temple is accomplished through the working of the charismatic graces.

Thus, the Lord in person is present and manifest through the ministry of the word. Through the various word gifts he invites, exhorts, consoles, admonishes, instructs, and gives explicit directions for building community.

Likewise, he manifests himself and pours out his other gifts to those who acclaim his presence in using the praise gifts.

And through the great charisms of priestly power, the Lord gives his very Person in his Eucharistic body and blood.

He is present and manifest also in the ministry to sinners, and in ministries to the ignorant, the sick, the anguished, the poor and the needy.

He is present too in the fellowshipping, the playing together inspired by his Spirit and love, as well as in the various services which contribute to this fellowshipping.

In some way or other, then, all the charismatic ministries or services are ordered to building up the body of Christ as a temple, a perfect milieu for experiencing the presence of the Lord and enjoying the uncreated grace. The many services rendered, whether hidden or obvious, work together for the peace and order of the community. Only in love's order can God's presence be fully enjoyed without worry and distraction, and without the confusion and divisions caused by sin. His presence can be fully perceived and appreciated only when we are at peace within ourselves and at peace with one another in love. Ultimately, all the unity and order brought about in the body through the charismatic gifts is for the sake of this peaceful joy in the presence of the Lord.

Thus, through the charismatic graces, the Lord builds up his body, not simply as an instrument he wishes to use in his work, but as a "place" where God is to be contemplated, appreciated, enjoyed! The charisms build the body of Christ into a temple in the sense that they vitalize its powers and focus the attention of its members on the person of God who dwells in it to be worshiped and appreciated for what he is in himself. We are the living stones of this temple, in lively communion with God and with one another.

The living temple is most "operative" in times of community worship, when, through the charisms, the whole community is aroused to explicit attention to the Lord who is present in its midst. But the body is a temple at all times, for recognition of the Lord and response to him when he manifests himself in everyday life are also worship. Thus, we praise the Lord each time we detect his workings in our own life or in the lives of others. Thus our life becomes a living temple of praise.

This living communication and exchange with God and with one another through the charisms are an expression and manifestation of our communion in the very love and life of the three divine Persons. We are built into a holy temple in the Lord, a dwelling place of God in the Spirit (cf. Eph 2:21ff.).

The highest perfection of the living temple comes about through the graces of infused contemplation, in which the Lord, dwelling in the deepest depths of our being, which he has entered through the sacrament of Baptism, and has entered anew and more profoundly through Eucharistic communion, manifests himself in our hearts by his very presence there. "I will love him and manifest myself to him. . . . We will come to him and make our home with him" (Jn 14:21, 23).

Charismatic communities are becoming aware of and ever more interested in contemplation and contemplative prayer. This is to be expected, for charismatic graces, focusing our attention on the Lord in person, open us ever more fully to his self-manifestation in these deep interior graces of contemplation. Community praise of the Lord and singing in the Spirit terminate more and more frequently in a deep interior silence of the heart, in which God's presence is deeply relished.

This is a normal development which comes about in fervent community prayer of praise. God's people begin to hunger for quiet and solitude to relish and appreciate the Lord Jesus, who wills to manifest himself to them by giving himself ever more intimately to them, along with the Father and the Holy Spirit, in the uncreated grace. "We will come to him and make our home with him" (Jn 14:23).

Part 7

Bride of Christ

Chapter 22

Receiving God's Touch

The uncreated grace, God himself dwelling in the deepest substance of our being, manifests his presence in us at times by perceptible "touches." God gives these when he pleases to give them, and especially to those who are prepared to receive them by their total submission to him in self-sacrificing love.

In persevering prayer, we learn to become ever more receptive to these touches. Prayer is much more than listening to God. It is receiving God himself into our hearts. For the fullness of what God wants to communicate to us cannot be expressed in words. It can be expressed only by the touch of his lasting presence in the depths of our heart.

Prayer is often described as conversation with God. Conversation, however, is not simply an empty exchange of words. If it is truly a listening and a responding, it results in true communication. We communicate with one another for various reasons. An employer, for example, communicates with his employees for the sake of their cooperation with him in work. Conversation and communication at their best, however, are not simply for the sake of cooperation in activity. They are for the sake of communion in love and life.

Communion in love and life requires the mutual revelation of hearts. One of the noblest purposes of conversation is self-revelation in love. Without self-revelation, a truly deep communion in love and life is not possible.

Ultimately, the purpose of all speech is communion in love and life. For man is destined for communion with God and communion with all his fellowmen.

When God speaks his words to men, it is for the sake of self-revelation and communion. "In many and various ways God spoke of old to our fathers by the prophets; but in these last days he has spoken to us in his Son" (Heb 1:1). The Son, who is ever in God's heart, is the Word in whom God reveals his heart to men. "No one has ever seen God. But God's only Son, he who is nearest to the Father's heart, he has made him known" (Jn 1:18).

The Son himself is God's Word to men. All that Jesus is and does speaks God to us. For God speaks more by doing than by saying. "God so loved the world that he *gave* his only Son" (Jn 3:16). This giving of his Son is his way of speaking to us, his way of revealing his heart. The giving of the Son as incarnate Word and in the sacrifice on the cross reveals God's love to us and offers it to us.

But this revelation and offer of love in the giving of the Son on the cross are only the beginning, only an invitation calling us to receive an ever more intimate revelation of God's heart.

The incarnate Word as incarnate is inadequate to express what God has to say to us. For what God did in sending his Son and giving him for us on the cross is still something outside you and me. Only when the Word touches us interiorly by his personal presence in our hearts can we really know God and be in communion with him in love. Only interiorly in our hearts is the Word fully manifest to us (Jn 14:21). To see him visibly in the flesh with our eyes, to hear the sound of his voice in our ears, is not enough. Only by an interior word of grace in the heart, a word which is indeed the touch of the Word's own presence in the heart, can we know him for what he really is, and in knowing him, know the Father also.

This is clear from Christ's response to Peter's profession of faith, "You are the Christ, the Son of the living God" (Mt 16:16). Jesus replied, "Flesh and blood has not revealed this to you, but my Father who is in heaven" (16:17). You know me as God's Son, Peter, only because you have had an interior illumination directly from God. You have had the direct touch of God in your heart. "No one can come to me unless the Father who sent me draws him" (Jn 6:44).

The prayer of believing, then, is more than listening to God's word in faith and responding to him in praise and petition. The prayer of believing, in its fullness, is receiving a touch from God. It is receiving a presence, a person, into our heart. For God gave his Son not just in the incarnation and not just on the cross. He gives him to each person who receives him by believing in him.

Believing is receiving. "To all who received him, by believing in his name, he gave power to become children of God" (Jn 1:12). Believing in his name is receiving the Son of God for what he really is. It is receiving the grace of divine sonship in him. Believing is receiving his indwelling presence. "If a man loves me, he will keep my word, and my father will love him, and we will come to him and make our home with him" (Jn 14:23). Believing is receiving the touch in which he manifests his presence in us. "I will love him and manifest myself to him" (Jn 14:21).

It is not enough then just to listen to God's words. Words cannot adequately express what God wishes to communicate to us. God can express himself adequately only in the interior touch of the Word dwelling in person in our heart.

That is why we said that the incarnate Word as incarnate is inadequate to express God. As visible and tangible to eyes and touch, the incarnate Word is only a sacrament, a sign and invitation, calling us to open ourselves in faith to receive a more profound inner revelation through his presence dwelling in our hearts. Only as entrusted to our hearts and interiorly received can the Word be an adequate revelation of God.

This seems to be the significance of these words in John's gospel: "Jesus would not trust himself to them, because he knew them all. . . . He was well aware of what was in man's heart" (Jn 2:24). Jesus did not trust himself to them, he did not give himself interiorly into their hearts, for their faith was still defective. At that stage, their faith was nothing more than a desire for miracles, for external works of God (cf. Jn 2:23; 4:48; 6:30). The believing that Jesus desires, so that he can do his interior work of revealing God in our hearts, is the total surrender of our person to him as Son of God and word of interior revelation. Only when he trusts himself to our hearts and is interiorly received can he adequately reveal the unseen God to us.

To this he calls us, invites us, alerts us when he shows his incarnate presence and addresses us by his word.

Already in the Old Testament, God's word was a sign of God's presence. When the Lord first spoke to the boy Samuel, the boy did not recognize that it was the Lord. But Samuel soon learned to recognize not only the Lord's word, but the Lord's presence manifested in the word. Speaking a word implies the presence of the speaker. Therefore it is written in the story of Samuel's vocation as a prophet, "The Lord came and *revealed his presence, calling out* as before, 'Samuel, Samuel!' " (1 Sm 3:9).

The Lord's presence is revealed in his word. Samuel does not see Yahweh, he hears him, for in his word Yahweh is really present with him. Samuel answers the Lord's call, "Speak, Lord, for your servant is listening" (3:10). But the prayer of listening, we said, is more than attentiveness to words. It is not simply being alert to words heard with the ears and understood with the heart. It is not just a matter of grasping the inner concept conveyed in the words. It is a listening to the inner word which is God's presence in the heart. The prayer of listening, the prayer of receiving, in its fullness, is detecting the delicate gentle touch of the Word's personal presence in our heart.

The Son's entrusting himself to the believing heart is the giving which is the completion of the Father's giving of his Son in the mystery of the incarnation and of the cross. The paschal mystery of cross and resurrection is completed only when the Son gives his Spirit into our hearts and manifests himself in our hearts by the working of this Spirit. The Spirit's work in our hearts is completed only when he has led us into the whole truth (Jn 16:13), only when he has fully revealed to us the Son and the Father. "He will glorify me, for he will take what is mine and declare it to you. All that the Father has is mine; therefore I said that he will take what is mine and declare it to you" (Jn 16:14-15).

The Word and his Spirit work as one in our heart, and the Father works as one with them. The three are inseparable from one another. Together, Son and Spirit bring us into the heart of the Father, the Father who is the source of their action, the Father who gives the Son and Spirit into our hearts.

O divine hand (the Father) you have wounded me in order to cure me . . . contacting me with the touch of the splendor of your glory and the figure of your sub-

stance (Heb 1:3) which is your only-begotten Son.
Through him who is your substance you touch mightily
from one end to the other (Wis 8:1). Your only-
begotten Son, O merciful hand of the Father, is the
delicate touch by which you touched me with the force
of your cautery (the Holy Spirit, the living flame) and
wounded me (John of the Cross, *The Living Flame of
Love,* stanza 2:16).

I did not need the witness of John of the Cross to con-
vince me of the realities of which we have been speaking.
Two young women, independently of each other, recently
witnessed to their personal incipient experience of these
realities, and inspired me to write about these things.

One of these women, just turned 20, and beginning
to experience the interior touch of the Word, wrote to me
wonderingly, seeking verification of what seemed to be
happening:

> One other thing that I think I've learned, but I'm not
> sure if it's valid (but I think it is). That, as you get
> more deeply into Christ, his relationship with you, his
> communication, his very *touch,* gets finer and finer.
> More delicate, and definitely more precious. But also,
> more subtle? You, on the other end, have to be more
> finely tuned to listen and *be* touched. Does that make
> sense?

Yes!

Only two weeks before this, another young woman, in
her later 20's, spoke to me of the Lord's touch in her heart.
She had never read John of the Cross either. At my recom-
mendation she began to read *The Living Flame of Love.*
She was delighted to find there the verification of what God
was doing in her heart. She was confirmed in her whole-

hearted desire to be ever alert to the touch of the Word, the touch which *is* the Word. And the touch of the Word is the touch of the very substance of God. For the Word is the brightness of his glory and the figure of his substance.

A listening heart, then, is a touchable heart, ever sensitive to the delicate interior touch of the Word. For what God wants to communicate to us cannot be expressed in words, but only by the touch of his permanent presence in our hearts. To this touch I must become ever more sensitive, sensitized by vivid faith in God's love for me personally, God's love bestowed upon me in his beloved Son.

It is not just a matter of listening to God's word in the scriptures or in the liturgy, but of surrendering my whole living person to the Person of the Word, that he might live in me by his Spirit and manifest himself to me (Jn 14:21). Only to the extent that I entrust myself to him can he entrust himself to me. Only to the extent that he entrusts himself to me can I appreciate and enjoy him.

Come, Lord Jesus! Only when you manifest yourself, only when you are the substantial touch in the deepest substance of my being will your work in me be nearing its completion. Come! "The Spirit and the Bride say, Come! Let each one who hears say, Come, Lord Jesus!" (Rv 22:17,20).

Chapter 23

Bride of Christ

The entire bible is summed up in its last words, "The Spirit and the Bride say, Come! Come Lord Jesus!" (Rv 22:17,20).

Not only the Christian community as a whole is the bride of Christ, but so is each individual member of the community. Therefore John adds immediately, "Let each one who hears say, Come!"

The bridal relationship of each Christian with the Lord is each one's direct personal union with the Word himself, who dwells in each one's deepest heart. The whole of God is given to each person in the community—not one part of God to you, and another part of God to me. God has no parts. He gives himself whole and entire to each one who surrenders himself wholeheartedly to him in faith and love.

This direct union of each Christian with the Lord is so intimate that God could find nothing else to compare it with except bridal union. This union is the deepest essence of the life in the Spirit.

St. Paul too, like the author of Revelation, speaks of the whole Christian community, and of each individual

Christian, as virgin bride of Christ. Paul writes to the whole community at Corinth, "I feel God's own jealousy for you, since I have given you in marriage to Christ, presenting you as a chaste virgin to this one husband" (2 Cor 11:2). But he speaks also of each individual's union with Christ in terms of bridal union.

When a man unites with a woman, he says, the two become one flesh. When Jesus unites himself with a believer, the two become one spirit (1 Cor 6:16-17). For when a believer surrenders himself to Jesus in faith and love, Jesus pours his own Holy Spirit into that person, and Jesus and the believer become one spirit in the Holy Spirit. "He who clings to the Lord becomes one Spirit with him" (1 Cor 6:17). This is clearly bridal imagery, for the Greek word translated as "clings" is the same word used in the Greek version of Genesis in speaking of the union of husband and wife: "A man leaves father and mother and clings to his wife, and the two of them become one body" (Gn 2:24).

In Paul's teaching, then, each individual believer, as well as the Church as a whole, is bride of Christ. The bridal metaphor expresses the intimacy of each one's direct union with the Lord.

This direct union with the Lord is the source of our union with one another in community. We are one in the Lord. Together, we come ever more intimately into the Lord. The transforming union of each and of all with him is the goal of Christian life. Nothing short of each one's total union with God is the purpose of Christian community, and only in union with him is our union with one another perfected.

Celibacy as Charismatic Witness

Christian celibacy is striking witness to this fundamental truth, that each Christian belongs totally to the Lord as

bridegroom. Each is called to possess him in the most intimate union possible. Each is called to transforming union,
in which God so possesses and penetrates the human person that he is completely divinized, transformed with God's
glory, possessing God completely in a marvelous personal
union.

All this is accomplished in Christ's body, the community. In his community, Jesus is not simply the first among
many brothers and sisters. He is our brother, but he is also
our Lord God. He does not simply hold first place in the
life of each, he *is* our life. Each is totally possessed by him
and each is destined to possess him totally. "I belong to my
beloved and he belongs to me" (Sg 3:8).

Therefore the Lord is the total focus in every Christian's life. Husbands and wives, parents and children,
friends and enemies are seen only in that focus. Jesus is
the total focus, because he is our life and he is our love. In
his love we love all others. With his love we embrace them.
He it is whom we want for them, just as we want him for
ourselves. We desire that he live in them and they in him,
just as we ourselves live in him and he in us. That is the
supreme desire of all love and friendship in the Holy Spirit.
"The Spirit and the Bride say, Come! Let each one who
hears say, Come!"

In letting Christ be my Lord and bridegroom, I make
him the center of my attention. No longer do I desire to
play lord, winning attention for myself as the center of attraction. I want only him to shine in my own heart and in
the hearts of all those whom I love. I do not want to possess
anyone exclusively for myself. I want the Lord to possess
them and fill them with his glory. Friends in Christian
community do not focus just on one another; together, they
focus on the Lord.

Celibacy in Charismatic Renewal

Perhaps the most heartening thing about the charismatic renewal is this recovery of direct focus on the Lord Jesus, and complete surrender to him to be filled with his transforming Spirit. The basic acclamation of the charismatics is, "Jesus is Lord!" (1 Cor 12:3).

Because they are yielding themselves to the Lord, they are in his hands, and he is completely transforming their hearts and their lives. He is healing all their relationships, he is restoring their marriages and families. But at the same time that he is restoring marriage to its full Christian holiness, the Lord is also calling certain persons in these charismatic communities to celibacy for the sake of the kingdom (Mt 19:22).

The phenomenon of consecrated celibates among the charismatics, existing in close connection with family and community restoration, confirms the truth affirmed by Vatican II, that consecrated virginity and celibacy will always be at the heart of the Church, witnessing to every Christian's call to direct intimacy with the Lord.

Celibacy rightly lived is a grace of charismatic witness, proclaiming a prophetic message to all Christians, and throwing light on the deepest reality of the Christian life: that grace of bridal union with the Lord, toward which every other grace and charism is directed.

Thus we see again the deepest reason for our profound reverence for each and every human person. Each one is called to a personal union with God so intimate that it is called bridal. In every human relationship, we let the other belong to the Lord! "He who has the bride is the bridegroom. The friend of the bridegroom, who stands by and hears him, rejoices greatly at the bridegroom's voice. Therefore this joy of mine is now full. He must increase, but I must decrease" (Jn 3:29).

Every Christian's Spiritual Celibacy

"There cannot be many in the Church who are physically virgins" (that is, virgins consecrated to the Lord), says St. Augustine, "but spiritually every one of the faithful should be a virgin" (*PL* 39:1496).

Spiritual virginity or celibacy, according to the Fathers of the Church, consists in the purity and integrity of the faith, in which each Christian belongs totally to the Lord Jesus, espoused to him in faithfulness to his word, entirely focused upon him, the bridegroom.

The concept of spiritual celibacy is rooted in the Sacred Scriptures. In the Old Testament, God's unfaithful people were described as having "a spirit of harlotry" (Hos 4:12). In the New Testament, by contrast, all faithful Christians are symbolized as virgins who "follow the Lamb wherever he goes" (Rv 14:4).

The bridal union of each Christian directly with Christ in faith is exemplified perfectly in Mary at the Annunciation. Through faith in the word of God, Mary "found the Word of God in the very bosom of the Father, and drew him into herself with her whole heart" (St. Ambrose).

"Letting Him Alone"

St. Joseph's relationship with Mary his wife exemplifies another aspect of the spiritual celibacy of all Christians.

Celibacy is not only a direct relationship with God, but is also a way of relating with every other person whom we love. The word "celibacy" derives from words meaning "to live alone." The consecrated celibate is "alone with the Lord," abstaining from marriage for his sake. The spirit of celibacy in my relationship with another means "letting him alone," letting him be himself, the true self God meant him to be, not manipulated and molded by me. It is the opposite of the possessiveness in which I try to be lord over him, using him for my own selfish purposes.

True love never uses the other person, but only promotes his true good, allowing him to be, and helping him to be, his true self. That self is the self the Lord wants him to be, the self the Lord is bringing him to be, leading him by his Holy Spirit.

This is exemplified in Joseph's relationship with Mary. The angel of the Lord said to him, "Joseph, son of David, do not fear to take Mary your wife, for that which is conceived in her is of the Holy Spirit" (Mt 1:20). Joseph accepted his wife in the spirit of celibacy, in profound reverence for the Holy Spirit's work in her. Obviously Mary belonged totally to the Lord, and Joseph's celibacy in relationship with her consisted essentially in letting her be the Lord's, rejoicing in what the Lord was accomplishing in her.

The spirit of celibacy as expressed in relationships with others, then, is basically a profound reverence for the other person, letting him be his true self, letting him be the Lord's. This spirit must govern all Christian relationships, whether with husband or wife, with parents or children, with strangers or with friends.

The Spirit of Celibacy: Focus on the Lord

The spirit of celibacy as a relationship with God is total focus on the Lord. As a relationship with others, it is reverence for them as belonging to the Lord, and joy in what the Lord is accomplishing in them through his Holy Spirit. The spirit of celibacy in our love for others focuses primarily on what the Lord wants the other to be, rather than upon what we would like the other to be for us.

This spirit, for example, should characterize the attitude of parents toward their children. We recall the story of Jacob's favorite son, Joseph. When Joseph told of his dream, "I have dreamed another dream; and behold, the sun, the moon and eleven stars were bowing down to me," not only were his brothers upset, but so was his father Jacob. At first Jacob rebuked the boy, "Shall I and your mother and your brothers indeed come to bow ourselves to the ground before you?" (Gn 37:9ff.). But the scriptures add immediately, "His brothers envied him, while his father pondered the matter" (Gn 37:11).

This reminds us of Luke's statement about Mary: "Mary kept all these things, pondering them in her heart" (Lk 2:19). She saw that God was working in a marvelous way in her Son. Jacob, too, was beginning to realize that God was at work in Joseph, and God's work must be reverenced. The boy must be allowed to be what God wills him to be.

The spirit of celibacy, or reverence for the Lord and what he is doing in their children, saves parents from possessiveness which hampers their children's growth. The celibate spirit focuses primarily on the Lord and his purposes in the loved ones.

The same spirit must characterize all who exercise leadership in a community. That too, says St. Paul, characterizes Christian love of husband and wife (Eph 5:25). If Christ's love for his Church purifies her in Baptism for total union with him, so husband reverences his wife as belonging to the Lord, destined for transforming union with him.

This is what Paul means when he says that "in the present distress" (1 Cor 7:26), "let those who have wives live as though they had none . . . for the form of this world is passing away" (7:29-30). The world is undergoing a transformation in union with the risen Christ, and all else will pass away. In the new age there will be no marriage; all will be united directly to the Lord.

In saying, "Let those who have wives live as though they had none," Paul is not retracting what he had said earlier in the same chapter when he told husbands and wives to fulfill their obligation of sexual union. He is simply telling them to do this within the greater context of their higher destiny to direct union with the Lord, reverencing one another as the Lord's own, not in bodily celibacy, but in the spirit of celibacy. We all belong to the Lord, and even love for each other must be an expression of love for him to whom we belong.

Belonging to one's wife or husband is a sacramental symbol of belonging to the Lord: "This is a great mystery" (Eph 5:32). For the intimacy of marital union is a symbol and pledge of the intimacy of total union with the Lord.

But when that great reality comes, the symbol of it will pass away. When the hidden reality of our life with God is revealed (Col 3:3), there will be no more need for signs or sacraments of the hidden reality. "For in the resurrection they neither marry nor are given in marriage" (Mt 22:30). Sexual union will pass away, but this does not mean that love will pass away. We will continue to love in a special way in heaven those whom we loved in a special way on earth, and in whose love we were helped to the Lord.

On earth we need the spirit of celibacy. We must be totally surrendered to the Lord if we are to be presence of the Lord and his love to our wife or husband, to our children and our friends, to our brothers and sisters in the community, to all our fellowmen, "the brothers for whom Christ died" (1 Cor 8:11).

Since letting others belong to the Lord involves a dying to self, celibacy is a mystery of dying with Christ for those for whom he died, that all might be the Lord's. This is the spirit expressed by Paul when he said, "If we are beside ourselves, it is for God; if we are in our right mind, it is for you. For the love of Christ impels us, because we are convinced that one has died for all; therefore all have died. He died for all, that those who live *might live no longer for themselves, but for him,* who for their sake died and was raised" (2 Cor 5:13-15).

In the spirit of celibacy, each one's direct personal relationship with the Lord must always be safeguarded. This personal relationship of each with the Lord is always fundamental in community. Each one is called to be the Lord's bride. "Abide in me," says the Lord (Jn 15:4), live in direct union with me, and you will be fruitful in my body, the community. Love for one another is the fruit which we bear when we abide in Christ. We cannot bear this fruit apart from him, just as the branches can do nothing from the vine (Jn 15:5). Even to love husband or wife in the Christian way, one has to be bride of Christ, abiding in him. The more deeply we abide in the Lord in love, the more fruitful we are in community love.

Christian celibacy is striking witness to this necessary direct union of each with the Lord.

Part 8

Growth in the Spirit

Chapter 24

Signs of Enduring Life in the Spirit

Community in the Lord is maintained only through daily reconciliation, for we are still sinners in the process of being redeemed. The Redeemer's work in us is not yet finished. Conversion is an ongoing thing, for we fall again and again. Yet through it all, the Lord and his Spirit continue in our midst, calling us anew to repentance, and preserving us from sin in the midst of severe temptation, as we carry on the spiritual combat.

The present chapter was written in response to the disappointment often expressed by members of charismatic communities when they discover that the experience called "baptism in the Spirit" has not brought them instantaneous impeccability and complete sinlessness.

The "baptism in the Spirit" is the experience of a deep conversion to the Lord, and often brings great fervor and enthusiasm in living the life of holiness. But then the first fervor wears off, and once again I begin to experience my weakness in the face of temptation, and perhaps I even fall again into my former sins. Therefore I may be tempted to think that my first enthusiasm in the Spirit was only an illusion, and that the Spirit is not with me after all.

Or perhaps on the contrary I stubbornly hold on to my conviction that the experience of the Holy Spirit has made me a saint, and in spiritual pride I refuse to accept the responsibility for the sins into which I fall afterwards. I put all the blame on Satan, instead of accepting myself as the sinner I still am, still in the process of being healed by Jesus to whom I have given myself as my personal Savior.

Blaming others is one of the characteristics of a sinner. He tries to explain his sin away, he tries to put the blame for his failings anywhere but on himself. Thus, when Aaron was questioned by Moses just after he had committed idolatry by making the golden calf, Aaron threw the blame on the people: "You know this people, that they are prone to evil" (Ex 32:22). Aaron would not accept the responsibility, nor even admit that he himself was one of these people who are so prone to evil.

So too Adam put the blame for his sin on Eve, instead of confessing his guilt. Even though Eve had enticed him, he was nonetheless personally responsible for his sin. He even blamed God: *You* gave me this woman! "The woman whom you put here with me, she gave me fruit from the tree, and so I ate it" (Gn 3:12).

Eve in turn blamed the serpent. We are all only too ready to blame Satan, when we ourselves are to blame. Our sins spring from our own sensuality, or pride, or malice, or weakness, or slothful lack of generosity toward the Lord and each other. Satan, of course, tempts us through these roots of sin which are within us. But we ourselves must accept the responsibility for our sins.

Sin brings ever-deepening separations among us. We turn against those with whom we have sinned, and put the blame on them. Only confession of our personal guilt, and the acceptance of responsibility for our sins, can prepare the way for reconciliation and the restoration of community.

I must put the blame for my sins where it belongs: on myself and on the roots of sin still embedded within me. One of the authentic signs of the Holy Spirit's presence within me is my humble admission that I am a sinner, trusting not in my own righteousness, but in the Lord's redeeming mercy. I *do* admit my guilt, for I am convicted by the Holy Spirit, who shows me myself as I really am.

Therefore when the first fervor of my "baptism in the Spirit" passes away, and I realize that I am a sinner, I need to be saved from disillusionment and discouragement. I need the more profound signs that the Holy Spirit is still with me, lest I give in to self-condemnation and discouragement.

As we shall see from the scriptures, my very acceptance of responsibility for my sins, and my perseverance in carrying on a courageous spiritual combat against the roots of sin within me, can be signs of a deeper life in the Spirit than are the charismatic graces which I may be exercising for the good of the community. Of themselves, the charismatic graces are not necessarily a sign that the person who exercises them is deeply holy.

In this chapter, therefore, we shall speak of some of the signs of the inner life in the Spirit, the more enduring signs of his presence in our very heart, rather than of the charismatic gifts which are the signs of the Spirit's activity in building up the community. For while the charisms manifest that the Spirit is working in the community, building it up, the signs that we shall now consider manifest that this individual or that one really is living the life in the Spirit. They show that the Spirit of Christ truly does dwell in a person in this deeply interior way.

These signs of the interior life in the Spirit are treated in Romans Eight and in the First Letter of John. John's letter, in fact, is nothing but a series of signs by which we can know whether we are in communion with God in the Holy Spirit. Neither Romans Eight nor First John has a word to say about the charismatic graces; they deal rather of the deeper essence of the life in the Spirit.

"Growing Pains" in the Spirit

From the first moment that God pours out his love into my heart by giving me his Holy Spirit of adoption as son, I am at home with God my Father. For I am loved and accepted by him, and through the witness of the Spirit in my heart, I know that I am loved by him. "The Spirit himself bears witness along with our spirit that we are sons of God" (Rm 8:16). The first sign, then, that the Holy Spirit is in me is my loving recognition of God as my Father.

But I show myself a son of God, and therefore that the Spirit is in me, not simply by saying "Father" (Rm 8:15) or "Lord" (1 Cor 12:3), but by living as God's son, doing always the will of the Father. "Not everyone who says to me 'Lord, Lord' shall enter the kingdom of heaven, but he who does the will of my Father" (Mt 7:21). "By this we may be sure that we know him, if we keep his commandments" (1 Jn 2:3). To know God means to acknowledge him not only in word, but in loving service. I must show that I am God's son by the way I live.

I have to go through "growing pains" in coming to full maturity in my divine sonship. Throughout all this growth, even when there is regression through sin, the Lord continues to be with me through the presence of his Holy Spirit. When I still stumble and fall in my weakness, my Father quickly acknowledges me again as his son, stooping to me in love, giving me the Holy Spirit anew in answer to my trusting cry for mercy and forgiveness. He receives me, the prodigal, by pouring his love anew into my heart, drawing me back to himself in my loving contrition, and renewing me in his love (Zep 3:17).

Recognition of My Sinfulness

It is his Holy Spirit in my heart who inspires me to acknowledge my sinfulness and turn in loving contrition to my
Father's mercy and love. The first sign that John gives that
I am "in the light" (1 Jn 1:7) and that therefore God's
Spirit dwells in me, is my recognition of myself as a sinner,
and my confessing my sinfulness. "If we say we have no
sin, we deceive ourselves, and the truth is not in us. If we
confess our sins, he is faithful and just, and will forgive our
sins and cleanse us from all unrighteousness" (1 Jn 1:8ff.).

John shows, too, how God himself works in the heart
that is troubled by its sinfulness. "God is greater than our
hearts, and he knows everything" (1 Jn 3:20). John says
this to reassure me when my conscience is troubled (3:19).
I am to take refuge in the very God I have offended.

God knows my heart not simply in the sense that nothing escapes his scrutiny. He knows my heart in the sense
that he works in it and lovingly draws forth from it my
faith and trust in his forgiving love. This is evident in the
scene showing the risen Jesus with the repentant Peter. The
same John who says that God is greater than our hearts
and knows all things, reports the response of Peter to Jesus,
"Lord, you know all things, you know that I love you" (Jn
21:17). You know my heart.

Peter's words throw light on the text, "God is greater
than our hearts." Throughout John's gospel, we see how
Jesus works in and "knows" the hearts of those whom he
draws to himself. Though he knows they are sinners, he
lovingly brings forth faith and love from these hearts. The
very repentance of the sinner is the fruit of the Lord's loving
knowledge of his heart and the power of the Lord's Spirit
lovingly poured into that heart. Three times the Lord questioned the heart of Peter who had denied him three times:
"Peter, do you love me?" (Jn 21:15-17). Knowing Peter

is a sinner, Jesus lovingly calls forth his love.

In the same way Jesus shows that he is greater than the Samaritan woman's heart and knows all things. "Go call your husband." "I have no husband." "You are right in saying you have no husband, for you have had five husbands, and he whom you have is not your husband" (Jn 4:16). "Come and see a man who has told me all that I ever did!" (4:29).

The three times that Jesus said to Peter, "Do you love me?" were all on the same occasion. But is not "three times" a symbolic number, indicating to me that even though in my weakness I fall many times, the God who knows my heart bends over this sinful heart again and again with his healing love, saying, "Do you love me?" He seeks my loving repentance. The very act of love in which I turn back to him in the Holy Spirit is the destruction of my sin and the healing of my heart. "You yourself are the remission of our sins," we used to say to the Holy Spirit in the old liturgy for the Tuesday of the Pentecost Octave (Postcommunion).

That God knows my heart means also that he acknowledges me anew as "the brother for whom Christ died." I respond anew, recognizing him anew as Father. The confidence with which I return to him in repentance is the work of the Holy Spirit in my heart, renewing and deepening in me my cry of acknowledgment, "Father!" Sincere contrition and repentance is the sign that the Holy Spirit is working in my heart.

Fraternal Love

According to John, fraternal love is the surest sign that the Holy Spirit dwells in me. Even when my conscience is troubled by temptations and by failures, John tells us that our authentic love for our brothers and sisters in Christ is a sign that we are in true communion with God. "Little children, let us not love in word or speech, but in deed and in truth. By this shall we know that we are of the truth, and reassure our hearts before him whenever our hearts condemn us; for God is greater than our hearts, and he knows everything" (1 Jn 3:18ff.).

St. Augustine has a magnificent comment on these words of John. "Question your heart, and if you find brotherly love there, set your mind at ease. Such love cannot exist without the Spirit of God." And he says it again: "By what does one get to know that he has received the Holy Spirit? Let him question his own heart. If he loves his brother, the Spirit of God dwells in him" (*PL* 35:2025).

Struggle Against Temptation

Not only my repentance for sins committed, but also my continuing struggle against temptation is the sign that God's Spirit is in me. "If by the Spirit you put to death the deeds of the body, you will live. For all who are led by the Spirit of God are sons of God" (Rm 8:13ff.). The man who lives in the Spirit is not amazed when he is tempted by "the flesh." His very persistence in struggling against the flesh is the sign that the Spirit of God is working in him. The flesh puts up resistance to the requirements of the Holy Spirit, but the Holy Spirit is persistent in his call and inspirations.

"The Spirit himself helps us in our weakness" (Rm 8:26), not simply the weakness of the body, still subject to suffering and death, but also the spiritual weakness of "the flesh," that is, our person as prone to the self-centeredness which is sin; whether it be sins of the spirit, such as pride and resentment, or sins of the passions, such as anger or lust. Since in this life we still have only "the first fruits of the Spirit" (Rm 8:23), not the final heavenly fullness of the Spirit, we still experience the weakness of the flesh to the extent that we are still only growing in the life in the Spirit, and have not yet let ourselves be totally possessed by him.

But the fact that by the Spirit I am putting to death the deeds of the flesh (Rm 8:13), hating them and rejecting them whenever they manifest themselves in me, is a sign that the Spirit is in me, even though at times I seem almost overwhelmed by weakness and sinfulness.

For it is the Spirit himself in my heart who makes me realize that my tendencies are evil, and causes me to hate the evil attraction which allures me so powerfully. An incident in the life of St. Catherine of Siena illustrates this strikingly. For several days Catherine was tortured by all sorts of obscene images whenever she tried to pray. She suffered intensely because of this. After several days of this torture, Jesus appeared to her. She promptly said to him, "Lord, where were you when I was so tortured by those images?" He replied, "Did you hate those things?" She answered vehemently, "Yes, Lord!" And he said, "Then I was in your heart all the time."

The very hatred of the evil which tempts me so powerfully is a sign of the presence of the Lord and his Spirit in my heart. The Spirit confronts me with "the flesh" in me. He lets me experience it so that I cry out to the Lord in hope. "In hope we are saved" (Rm 8:24). Even in my experience of myself as seemingly more flesh than spirit, I hope anyway, and cry out to the God who is greater than my heart, who dwells in my heart, carrying on his work of transforming me into the likeness of his Son.

Contemporary Witness to This

What happened to St. Catherine still happens. In a recent discussion on prayer, I was asked, "Why is it that when I pray, so much that is not from the Lord comes into my efforts to pray?" This person, who had experienced the "baptism in the Spirit," was used to receiving beautiful graces of prayer which definitely were of God. But she was referring now to temptations which flooded even into the midst of her prayer.

Even though these allurements to sin were "not from the Lord," as she put it, her sorrow for them, and her refusal to follow them, definitely were from God. We should recognize that God's presence in us can be manifest in sorrow for sin and in hatred of troubling temptations, as well as in prayer and praise in which we experience his closeness and love. Perhaps this is even a sign that he is closer to us than before, allowing us to experience our weakness and sinfulness so that our trust in his love will grow strong, and will open us to his purifying action.

It is not surprising that people who have enjoyed intimacy with God in prayer, and have tasted the sweetness of his presence, then go through a stage when they strongly experience their sinfulness and weakness. God's very presence in the heart shows up its sinfulness. The sign that God still "knows" such people as his own, and lovingly shows that he is greater than their hearts, is their act of humble abandon to his loving mercy, in humility and adoration and hope in his love.

Such trust can only be a response to him who knows them, accepting them in his Son. They are "in the light" (1 Jn 1:7); that is, in right relationship with God who is merciful love. "If we walk in the light . . . the blood of his Son Jesus cleanses us from all sin" (1 Jn 1:7).

Here is the testimony of another person (used with her permission), who for a long time had been experiencing joyous intimacy with God in deep interior prayer. But then. . .

I have really been experiencing my sinfulness these past weeks. This is hard to put into words. But my heart has felt so sad at its depths. I feel so unworthy of the Lord, so unfaithful and sinful. I am filled with impatience, I have gotten angry so many times, and so easily talk about the faults of others. I complain, judge others, and often so little remember his presence during the day. In my prayer, all I can do is just cast myself at his feet and with silent heart beg for his mercy. I feel so far away from him.

I'm not really completely sad. It's just that I feel gently the weight of God's love for me, and how I do not correspond.

I do not concentrate on this sadness. I turn everything into praise of him. This is a magnificent opportunity really to trust in his mercy. I am learning more and more through this the real mercy of God, and how concentration on our sinfulness really keeps us away from him.

How clearly I see how weak and nothing I am without him. He is letting me see that, and yet I dare to cast myself on his mercy, and continue to believe in the reality of all the wonderful things he let me experience before. But now I see his total magnificence, how glorious he is to do such things for someone who is so nothing! Jesus, I believe in your mercy!

This person's humble and repentant trust in the Lord's mercy was itself a precious prayer, and was as valid a sign that she was in communion with God in the Holy Spirit as were her previous prayers of praise and intimacy with God dwelling in her heart. Indeed, she came to realize that her previous warm experience of his loving presence was as much a work of his mercy to a sinner as was his later forgiveness of her sins. For that deep-rooted sinfulness had been there even during her earlier experiences of his intimacy.

She had the wisdom to see that she must not concentrate on her sadness and sinfulness. To do so would have been itself a sin, a sin against God's love and mercy, a sin against his Holy Spirit of love and joy who was impelling her to her Father, even while he was convicting her of her sinfulness. The very revelation of our sinfulness to us by the Holy Spirit working in us is simultaneously an invitation to turn lovingly and trustfully to the loving Father who is greater than our hearts.

Endurance in Hope

The witness of the Spirit dwelling in my heart impels me toward the Father in undying hope, even when my aspiration toward him is expressed as unutterable groanings from the depths of my weakness and from the darkness of my tribulations (Rm 8:26). This hope which perdures throughout my weakness, darkness, and even failures, is the sign that the Spirit is in me, even when I find it difficult to express my prayer in joyous praise. My long-suffering is itself praise, for it is my witness in the Spirit to God's undying, faithful love for me.

Even when I sin, the Spirit witnesses anew to my Father's faithful love for me, calling forth from my heart a new surge of hope. I reach up anew to receive the Father's embrace, as he welcomes me back as his prodigal child, coming to him in repentance.

Although this indestructible hope, the sign of the Spirit's presence in me, is often expressed as groanings and gropings, because we hope for the unseen (Rm 8:25), at other times it bursts forth in triumphant joy even in the midst of sufferings, because the victory is certain: "We rejoice in our hope of sharing the glory of God. More than that, we rejoice in our sufferings, knowing that suffering produces endurance, and endurance produces tested virtue, and tested virtue produces hope. And hope does not disappoint us, because God's love has been poured into our hearts through the Holy Spirit who has been given to us" (Rm 5:2-5).

God has acknowledged us as his sons, pouring the Spirit of the Son into our hearts. "Who shall separate us from the love of Christ?" That is, from Christ's love given to us, poured into our hearts in the gift of the very person of the Holy Spirit. In the most severe tribulations "we are more than conquerors because of him who loved us" (Rm 8:37). "I am sure that nothing in all creation will be able to separate us from God's love which comes to us in Christ Jesus our Lord" (Rm 8:39). Nothing can tear us from God's love given to us in his Son, nothing can tear us from our love in response. Our indestructible love for God, reaching up to him in the certitude of hope and trust, is possible only because his love actually dwells in us in the person of his Holy Spirit, who is the abiding interior witness to us of God's love. The Spirit bears witness to God's unshakable love for us by the unshakable love for God which he causes in our hearts.

I know that I have the Spirit, then, because I experience his presence in this effect which he produces in me: my enduring trust and love. Endurance in love is the sign of the Spirit's presence in my heart. It is a direct personal union of the Holy Spirit with my spirit. God's love for me and my love for him in response is one love in the Holy Spirit. It is loving communion with my Father in the Holy Spirit of his Son.

My endurance of sufferings in love is not a grudging, joyless endurance, but an endurance accompanied by joyous praise and thanksgiving. For I rejoice in the hope which cannot be disappointed, because it is the work of the Holy Spirit in my heart (Rm 5:4-5). He bears interior witness in my heart that I am son of God in Christ; and if son, then heir with Christ, but only if I suffer with him (Rm 8:16ff.). I must be united with him in the image of his sufferings if I would be united with him in the likeness of his glory (Rm 6:5; 8:29).

All this is the work of the Holy Spirit in me. I am in direct personal communion with him, and in him with Jesus and the Father. "He who clings to the Lord is one Spirit with him" because the Lord's own Holy Spirit dwells in his spirit (1 Cor 6:17).

Chapter 25

"He Shall Be My Son"

We began this book by telling about the woman at the prayer meeting who learned beautiful lessons about prayer while watching her husband bend over their infant's cradle. Our first cry to God in prayer, our repeated "Abba, Abba," is like the infant's first attempts to say "Daddy!" Our prayer may seem to us to be like an infant's babbling, but we must not be discouraged, for our Father is like the daddy bending over the crib, listening to us, patient with our efforts, inviting us on, drawing us to himself in his Holy Spirit. "We do not know how to pray as we ought, but the Spirit himself makes intercession for us with groanings that cannot be expressed in speech" (Rm 8:26).

We say that God listens to our prayers. In truth, he listens to something deeper than our prayers, just as an earthly daddy listens to something deeper than the child's words and whines and entreaties. A listening daddy interprets and responds to the child's true and deeper needs. Likewise our listening God, who hears our prayers, is ever attentive to the deepest needs of the human nature which he himself has given to us.

He listens above all, says St. Paul, to the desires which

his own Holy Spirit inspires in us (Rm 8:26). For the Spirit asks for us according to God's will (8:27); that is, according to God's loving purpose to conform us to the image of his Son (8:29), that we might receive the inheritance with the Son (8:17), and live in the fullness of loving communion with the Father.

When God's magnificent love wills to give us something, he himself stirs up in us the desire for it through his Holy Spirit. This loving desire opens us to receive it. Though we ourselves do not clearly know what we are desiring and asking (Rm 8:26), God, who searches the hearts of men (8:27), listening to hear their desires, rightly interprets these desires, for he himself has inspired them (8:27). He is greater than our hearts, and fashions them according to his loving purposes (Ps 33:15). He has had to inspire our desires, because what he wills to give us is beyond our imagining (1 Cor 2:9), and we could not even begin to desire it, if he himself did not inspire this desire.

If God thus listens to our hearts and to the desires which his Spirit inspires in them, we ourselves should listen to these inspirations of the Spirit, so that we might come to an ever-clearer understanding of what God's loving will wants to give us. In coming to this clearer understanding, we open our hearts in ever more enlightened desire for these better gifts. The quality of our response to the inspirations of the Spirit conditions what God's love is able to do in us.

For our listening Father never forces his will upon us. Rather, he invites our loving response. Christian obedience is loving cooperation with love. Our obedient response to our listening God is response to his invitation to work together with him in love. "We know that in everything God works for good *with* those who love him, who are called according to his purpose" (Rm 8:28). Christian obedience is not reluctant submission to a will imposed arbitrarily by authority. It is loving response to an invitation of love.

Growth in Divine Sonship

The most basic sign of our enduring life in the Spirit, we said, is our cry "Abba, Father," our response to God, reaching out to him in loving hope for his full embrace. Through the Spirit's presence in my heart, I am "known" by God, accepted as his son. "The Spirit himself bears witness along with our spirit that we are sons of God" (Rm 8:16).

The "power to become sons of God" (Jn 1:12), the power of the Holy Spirit given to us by Jesus, is a power to grow to full maturity in response to the Father's call. We are named "sons of God" to bring out that God gives us a sharing in his own life. "See what love the Father has given us, that we should be called children of God; and so we are" (1 Jn 3:1). As son, each of us responds directly to the Father in the Son and Spirit, thus entering into the intimate life of the Trinity. In Jesus, the Son, each is in intimate communion with the Father.

"He Shall Be My Son"

Even in the final fullness of God's people, the heavenly Jerusalem, the eternal Father will acknowledge and receive each single one of us personally. He will not receive us just as a huge mass of people in which the individuals are indistinguishable from one another in the crowd, he will address us not only in the general covenant formula of the Old Testament, "I will be their God, and they shall be my people" (Jer 31:33). He will adapt this formula to each one of us, he will address each in the singular, "I will be his God, and he shall be my son" (Rv 21:7). Emphasis on Christian community must never be allowed to cause de-emphasis of each one's unspeakable importance before God his Father.

As a whole people we are God's family because each single one of us is son in the Son. To each one of us, the Father speaks as to his only Son: "You are my beloved son, in whom I am well pleased" (Mt 3:17). We are all one in the Son, and yet no one of us ever loses his own distinctive personality. Each child of God is unique. The Lord Jesus is complete only in the multiplicity of his members, which is a unity in diversity. God's family is the multitude of his children, each one of whom is uniquely himself. The more distinctive and wonderful each child is, the richer and more beautiful the whole family is. It is very important for the fullness and richness of community in the Lord that each one be his distinctive self within the beautiful unity in love.

Last Stage of Growth in the Image

From the first instant of the Spirit's presence dwelling in our hearts, we recognize God as Father: "Abba!" Our last act of recognition of our Father in this life should be in the likeness of Christ's own joyous acknowledgment of his Father in the moment of his death, "Father, into your hands I commend my spirit" (Lk 23:46). The psalm which Jesus was praying in these last words continues: "Let me be glad and rejoice in your love. Blessed be the Lord who has shown me the wonders of his love" (Ps 30:5,7,21). This indicates that Christ's last words were a joyous response to his Father's love for him.

What we will be like, when the image of God in us is completed after this final total surrender to him in love, has not yet been shown to us. "Dearly beloved, we are God's children now. What we shall be later has not yet come to light. We know that when it comes to light, we shall be like him, for we shall see him as he is" (1 Jn 3:2). Seeing him as he is will be our full recognition of our Father, and therefore the fullness of our divine sonship.

If this side of the moment of death is the loving surrender of our whole being to God, "Father, into thy hands I commend my spirit," the other side of death is the astonished recognition of God our Father in the instant we see him face to face: "Father!" What a rapturous cry it will be! And he will say, "Son!"

We will recognize him, because we have always known him in our hearts since that first cry inspired in us by the Spirit when he was first given to us, "Abba!" Yet we will be astonished and enraptured when we see him face to face, for his glory and beauty and love and fatherhood are infinitely beyond anything we could ever have imagined: "No eye has seen, no ear has heard, no heart of man has conceived, what God has prepared for those who love him" (1 Cor 2:9).

When we see him face to face, no more will our prayer be like an infant's babbling attempts to reach his father. "Then I shall know him even as I am known" (1 Cor 13:12). To know, in biblical language, means "to experience in love." Heaven is not just a seeing. It is the full experience of God's life and love, and the full response to that love. It is the fullness of our sharing in the very life of the Holy Trinity. It is the fullness of sonship in the Son, the fullness of our response to the Father in the Son and his Holy Spirit. It is being fully at home with God, and with everyone in God's family.

All this has begun in us even now. "All the way to heaven is heaven, because he said, 'I am the Way'" (St. Catherine of Siena). We are on the way in the Son and in his body, the community. The Christian community, in the Acts of the Apostles, is called "the Way" (Acts 9:2; 22:4). The Way is already heaven on earth, for in the body of Christ, the Christian community, we already share in the communion of the three divine Persons.

Our whole destiny is to be, at last, fully at home in God.

Epilogue

The Community of God's Delight

As I was writing the last chapter of this book, and reflecting upon the distinctive personality of each son and daughter of God within the unity of God's family, I remembered that each person's uniqueness is expressed in the distinctive name by which the Good Shepherd calls him. "He calls his own sheep by name" (Jn 10:3). I thought of another text which seemed to express the same truth: "To him who conquers I will give . . . a new name . . . which no one knows except him who receives it" (Rv 2:17).

It seemed to me that the "new name" must signify each one's unique personality, for "no one knows it except him who receives it." But upon further investigation, I discovered to my delight that these words contain an infinitely more marvelous truth than that.

To receive the new name which no one knows except him who receives it is to share in that divine and mysterious name which Jesus received in the resurrection, "the name above every name" (Phil 2:9), the name of God, "a name which no one knows but himself" (Rv 19:12).

In Semitic thinking, a person and his name are consid-

236

ered to be somehow identical. The name is the person who bears it. God is the name which no one knows but himself. Only God knows God. Jesus shares fully in this knowledge of God, for he is God: "No one knows the Son except the Father, and no one knows the Father except the Son, and anyone to whom the Son chooses to reveal him" (Mt 11:27).

To receive the new name, the name of the risen Christ, is to be brought into the very person of the Son of God and to share in his divine life, and thereby to enter into the very life and nature of the Holy Trinity.

No one knows this name except him who receives it. That is, one can know this name, one can know God, only by receiving the name, receiving God's own life, living it, knowing and experiencing it in living it.

"On him who conquers I will write the name of my God, and the name of the city of my God, the new Jerusalem, which comes down from my God out of heaven, and my own new name" (Rv 3:12). The whole city of God, the entire family of God's people, and each individual member of that family, bears the name of God, lives the very life of the Holy Trinity!

All this had been announced beforehand through the prophet Isaiah: "You shall be called by a new name, which the mouth of the Lord shall give. . . . You shall be called 'God's Delight' " (Is 62:2-4).

God delights in Jesus, his beloved Son: "This is my beloved Son, in whom I am well pleased" (Mt 3:17). And God delights in each of his people, because he recognizes and acknowledges his own Son in each of them, for all are sons in the Son. Of each he says, "This is my beloved Son, in whom I am well pleased." And he delights in the whole family of his people, for they are all one in his Son. "You shall be called 'God's Delight' " (Is 62:4).

*   *   *   *

On that evening a year and a half ago when I was told that the charismatic community in Dallas is called "The Community of God's Delight," somehow I knew in a flash everything that I would write in this book, though it has taken a year and a half to put it into words. That initial insight was deepened when I heard the woman in the prayer meeting tell about her husband bending over their infant's cradle, and how from this she had learned so much about our heavenly Father's relationship with each one of us, his sons and daughters.

Perhaps some of my readers have been wondering why a book on community should put so much emphasis on each individual person and his intimate personal relationship directly with the Lord. I know that the book had to be this way, the more I saw manifest in the Dallas community God's deep concern not only for infants in the cradle, but his concern even for all the unborn persons still in their mothers' wombs. In his community in Dallas, God has emphatically manifested the sacredness of human life. He has wonderfully exerted his power in restoring family life, and in calling the little children to himself. He has asserted anew the inviolability of every single person, which is a fundamental truth of the gospel.

Reverence for persons is essential in community. There can be no community where there are no persons! God himself is community of Persons.

The Community of God's Delight has the mission to witness before everyone that God wills to do in all what he is doing in them.

*   *   *   *

That is why this book was written. In the spring of 1973, I was invited to participate as a theologian in a conference to consider the theological foundations of the charismatic renewal, to be held at the University of Notre Dame in July. Since authentic theology is reflection upon actual Christian experience in the light of the scriptures and tradition, I knew that I could make no contribution to such a discussion unless I knew profoundly what is happening among the charismatics in the Catholic Church. Therefore at once I became more deeply involved with the Community of God's Delight, and reflected on all that I saw and heard and experienced. This book is some of the fruit of this reflection. It is my way of sharing in that community's witness to what God wishes to do in all his people.

ACKNOWLEDGMENT

In writing this book, I received invaluable aid from Sister Mary Ann Fatula, O.P. She read the first draft of the book, and convinced me that I must completely rewrite it. The revised version is structured around key concepts which she presented. She is the one who said to me, "Community is 'being at home,' " "Home is where everyone listens," "A father is first of all a listener," "The key to community is appreciation," "Appreciation is akin to contemplation," "Prayer is appreciating God," "Community is people growing," and many other sayings which have become titles in the book. These titles indicate her profound influence on the book as a whole.

Chapter 10, "Whose Life Have I Touched?" was inspired by a Lenten prayer and penance service which she led in her religious community. She is responsible also for the way in which "Community Reconciliation" (Part V), is written. My original presentation of sin as destructive of community was too theological and abstract. When she read it, she flatly declared, "That is not how people experience sin." She promptly proceeded to present to me the basic concepts of Chapter 17, "Sin Destroys Community," and many of the ideas of Chapter 18, "The Sacrament of Community Reconciliation."

The book would not have been written without her urgings and encouragement which accompanied her devastating critique of the original draft.

I gratefully acknowledge my great indebtedness to her. Sister Mary Ann, a native of Pittsburgh, is a member of the Faculty of Scripture and Theology at Ohio Dominican College, Columbus, Ohio.

240